EMPOWERING WOMEN TO SUCCEED

EMPOWERING WOMEN TO SUCCEED

From Burnout to Victory

Randi Goodman

Lisa Bartello | Maria Grazia Bevilacqua
Sabbir Chawala | Marla David | Jennifer Douglas
Heather Gordon | Calli Jensen | Danielle Joworski
Natalie Marnica | Jenny McKaig | Lisa Rizzo
Ellie Savoy | Laura Vella | Minni Sharma

Empowering Women to Succeed
From Burnout to Victory

ISBN: 978-1-5331-6186-4
ASIN: B01EKIES64

Printed in Canada

CONTENTS

ACKNOWLEDGEMENTS

We created the first version of the book *Empowering Women to Succeed, Tough Times Don't Last But Tough Women Do*, so we could connect with you, the reader, on a personal level, and show you that you are not alone.

The journey of the authors to express themselves, to share their personal stories, to even think about writing it down on paper, is at minimum, a struggle personally. It is not an easy task to go back and relive some of the feelings and experiences we all have had in our lives.

I am in awe of the strength and power each of these women and man have and their desire to help you with your own struggles, connecting with you and aiding you in moving forward with your own lives.

Firstly, I would like to thank my business partner Gordon So, who has been an incredible mentor and supporter going through this process. It was his creativity that brought this book series to life in the first place, which has already helped so many around the world. You work tirelessly behind the scenes and in front and I appreciate every day all that you do for myself and entrepreneurs alike. You have a strong will to help others and I am honoured to have the opportunity to work so closely with you. Thank you too to Stephanie for being the wonderful life partner and wife to Gordon, and all that you do to give back to the community!

I would also like to thank Jenny McKaig and her team, Colin Hegarty and Linsey Fischer, who have worked tirelessly to put this awe-inspiring compilation together. They have been very professional and ensured that the final version of the book is professionally completed. I cannot thank them enough and want to recognize them for all of their hard work. I am so lucky to have such a dedicated editor, with such a strong team, who has worked non-stop, on this book — thank you Jenny and team!

Thank you Pasha Carter for everything you do for women and entrepreneurs all over the world. You have helped tens of thousands of people, mentoring them, helping them have their own success. I am honoured that you wrote the Foreword in our book and are an incredible friend.

I want to thank Jonathan Himelfarb for his continued support and surprise to the fact that we actually wrote a book (and now the second). This is a legacy that I leave to our children. Joey, Benny, Daniel and David are the shining light in my life. As teens and coming out of teenage-hood, you are strong young men who will make an impact on this world (well, more than you already have). I thank you for allowing me the time to write, for being there for me when I need you. It is you who keep me going, who raise my adrenaline to succeed and push forward. I appreciate you and love you. I thank the universe every day that I have you.

I would like to thank my brother Richard Goodman and sister Staci Goodman for being the rocks in my life. You are always there for me and I cherish my relationship with both of you more than you know. My gorgeous and brilliant Brooke and Cori are two shining stars. I love you all with all of my heart.

I miss all four of my grandparents who are no longer here. They are always with me in my heart and in my mind; I miss them dearly. You were always there for me, you allowed me to stay out late, let me eat junk food and an entire Challah and I love spending so much time with you. You were my saviours, my happiness, my joy. I really miss you all and think of you all the time; Kate and Joseph Goodman,

Sala and BerBlady (and Grumpy, that book is still coming, another step forward!).

Thank you to my mom, Mary Goodman, for helping me learn to release the pain I had inside as a child from holding in all those feelings. For always wanting to be there, even if I didn't appreciate it at the time. For wanting the best for Richard and I, for doing the best that you could under strenuous circumstances.

Thank you to my D.O.D. (Dear Old Dad), Phil Goodman, for mentoring me with invaluable conversation as a child and as an adult. You always treated me with respect, even as a child. Thank you for mentoring me indirectly as I watched you treat all with respect, regardless of their position within a company; be it janitor to V.P., you were and are a model of how a businessperson should treat others. Thank you for allowing me the opportunity to learn from you and gain business experience that I otherwise would not have the opportunity to know. It had more of an impact on me than you know. I love an appreciate both of my parents.

Thank you Linda for 'checking in' to catch up and see if there is anything you can do. You are a mentor yourself and help so many people. Thank you for all that you do for others. Zach, my younger brother (30 years younger), you have a great life ahead of you. You love to help others and have a desire to achieve. I love you both.

And, without mentioning more names, thank you to my close friends who are always there for me, regardless of what is going on in their lives. I love you, you mean more to me than you know.[*]

– Randi Goodman

[.] Some of the names have been changed in the stories to respect their privacy.

[*] *You will see two different spellings of God/G-d in this book. This is because of the different religions and we respect each and every one of them.

FOREWORD

I immediately knew from our very first conversation that Randi Goodman had her hands on something special that would change the lives of so many women. I had just flown across the continent to Toronto to be a keynote speaker at the Toronto Women's Expo, where hundreds of women from around the world gathered to learn, share and showcase their growing businesses and passions. I observed Randi's authentic passion to uplift and empower other women by giving them a platform to take their personal lives, their health and their businesses to the next level.

I was already familiar with Randi's first book, *Empowering Women to Succeed: Tough Times Don't Last but Tough Women Do*, which is a #1 international bestseller. Sharing the collective wisdom of women who have opened doors, overcome obstacles and passionately gone from failure to success without losing enthusiasm and without giving up on what's important in life is priceless. So when Randi started telling me about her new book, *Empowering Women to Succeed: From Burnout to Victory*, my heart skipped a beat because as a mom, a wife and a successful business owner, I know what it's like firsthand to go through immense pain and challenges on the road to success and happiness.

I've devoted myself for the past two decades to inspiring, empowering and transforming the lives of thousands of women around the world. As I travel the world and speak to thousands, so many women come to me and share their trials and what they consider to be their failures. They express how they sometimes question themselves, their lives, their beliefs, their businesses and even their sanity. What I have found is that many of these women feel that they are alone and that they are the only ones experiencing these challenges, which is so far from the truth. Every day in my trainings and coaching sessions, I see women that are struggling to get past what I call *the tests of life*. Like many of us, the women who share their journeys in this book had to dig deep to find light during their darkest moments.

Empowering Women to Succeed: From Burnout to Victory is a book that lets us inside the intimate lives of some of the most powerful women in the world as they pour out their hearts and share their stories. With every page turn and story unveiled, Randi Goodman and these courageous authors allow us to see up close and personal how to replenish our spirits and overcome our deepest pain through the experiences of these real life powerhouses.

When I read the chapters in this powerful, insightful and life-changing book, I was so moved by the life stories that lay between the pages. The first story I read was Ellie's, full of loss and grief. Her pain jumped off the pages and grabbed me, shaking me to my core. She reminded us that there is no rehearsal or preparation for the death of someone you love. She was so open and vulnerable and allowed us to experience her journey from pain to the realization that even our most difficult times don't have to rob us of our dreams and our well-being.

The beauty of this book is that Randi Goodman includes a diverse group of women and one man with unique circumstances and struggles. As you'll see in ***Empowering Women to Succeed: From Burnout to Victory***, the road isn't always an easy one. The pressure of juggling career, family obligations and tragedies and personal time can be challenging. Women like those in this book have truly opened up their hearts and bared their souls to teach us important life lessons that are often silenced.

Having ***Empowering Women to Succeed: From Burnout to Victory*** on your nightstand is like having an inner circle of girlfriends giving you encouragement on a nightly basis. There is always advice that every woman needs to keep going until she goes from burnout to victory. These women are proof that a setback is a setup for comeback!

Pasha Carter
Founder of Carter Leadership Development
www.PashaCarter.com

INTRODUCTION

Gordon So first came to me with a book cover and an idea. "Here is the book cover to the book we are going to write," he said, "*Empowering Women to Succeed: Tough Times Don't Last But Tough Women Do*." My first reaction, silently, was "oh my G-d we are going to write a book?"

It's so funny because my ex, Jon, is such an avid reader. He reads everything and absorbs it all. When I was in university, I would read halfway through a page in the textbook and fall asleep. I only liked to read one type of book and that was it. It had to be a real life story, no fiction, and I probably didn't remember half of what I read.

The process of going through the first book, with 16 authors, 15 women and one man, was exhilarating. I really never thought it would or could be done, let alone having *me* writing in a book!

Sixteen people sharing their stories, personal or professional, and sharing how they helped themselves and others, has a transformational effect on us all. When you read the stories, you not only enjoy the flow of the writing (thank you to Jenny and her team), but you also connect with the reader on a factual and emotional level. The process they share with you and some of the things they did to overcome obstacles, is priceless.

Each of the authors' stories revealed in the sequel to the first book, *Empowering Women to Succeed: From Burnout to Victory*, has resonated with me on every level. Each of their experiences have brought me to a higher level and I am thrilled to be able to spread their message around the world.

The driving force of this book and series is our utmost desire to help you, our reader. You may not resonate with every story, but you will be able to appreciate and see what each author overcame. Maybe, just maybe, you will share it with someone you know and help change their life for the better. Other stories you will resonate with, pull pointers from and impact your own life to take you to new heights!

Baring their all, in business, in friendship, in all relationships, these 15 authors bring together their experiences and expertise to show you that you are not alone, and there is support, no matter what you are going through. You can be happy and have the success you desire.

Empowering Women to Succeed: From Burnout to Victory is a book you can read at any time. It will shock you, it will bring tears to your eyes, a smile on your face. We have written it for you.

As the title author in the book, I am proud to say we have the most unbelievable stories shared by brilliant coaches, successful business owners, entrepreneurs, writers and non-writers alike, moms, a dad, actresses and healers.

Inside, you will read 15 personal stories that draw you in and make you feel like you are on that journey with each and every one of them. Each of these incredible people have unleashed their inner thoughts for the one purpose to show you that you can do it too; you can get through anything, regardless of the challenge, big or small.

Empowering Women to Succeed: From Burnout to Victory, although written for women, strives to help all people, including men, who will gain supreme knowledge from this book to enjoy success in their lives. This book is meant to give you tools and resources to open your mind, take steps, even baby steps, towards your success and enjoy a full and empowering life.

It is a choice you make to live the life you want. Our authors have made a choice and have taken steps to improve the quality of their lives; it is up to you to do the same. I look forward to you reading the stories and finding the one, or many, that help you get to make a shift in your life for the better. The authors' contact information is in the Bios and Resources section at the back of this book if you want to reach out to thank them for, or ask questions about, their story.

Be inspired, be motivated, there is a light at the end of the tunnel, not all is lost. I appreciate all of you and wish you success in everything that you do!

~Randi Goodman

PROLOGUE

Everything came together so perfectly. Freshly printed books were displayed for the sold out crowd who signed up to attend the ***Empowering Women to Succeed: Tough Times Don't Last But Tough Women Do*** book launch. Women and men alike all congregating together to support the 16 authors and to celebrate the success of women all over the world. The event was so fun and successful; it propelled the book to hit the international bestseller list on day one!

To say the process of getting that book and event together was easy would be a whopping fib. In total it took about five months of incredibly hard work. Trying to organize 16 people to make sure their drafts were in on time, working with them and the editing team to make sure each author felt fantastic with their chapter and that every chapter fit the theme, all while organizing more events, teaching at seminars and working with multiple clients on digital marketing and joint ventures—it took a lot out of me. My skills I learned through my event-planning experiences did help me a lot though. I work at lightning speed (says our editor Jenny), so whenever a problem arose, I faced it head on, determined to find and have a solution within minutes. If I didn't work like that, keeping my mindset focused on the best end results, I may have gotten caught up with what could be for many a stressful process. I believed in my vision and dream, however, and I believed in all the authors banding together to make an incredible book that would help people all over the world.

Two days before the book needed to go to print, there were challenges with a few of the chapters and a pressing deadline with the publisher.

I remember a few nights of a lot of coordination, fielding author calls and getting information for the final editing. One night in particular, Jenny McKaig, our senior editor, was working through the night to get every detail finalized so the book could be launched; I remember it clearly. I was on the phone with her (how could I sleep if she couldn't sleep?), supporting in every way I could, and on the phone with the printers, keeping them up to date with the status of everything so we could still make the deadlines and get the book to print. I believe in helping people, and supporting them, giving in whatever ways I can to make everything I work on—and the things others work on that they care deeply about—a great success.

Twenty-four hours after that night, where the book was in its final stages—and what could have been a very stressful situation—we looked over everything for the final time, and sent that baby off to press.

Was I tired at three in the morning when I would normally be sleeping? Yes. Did I find the resiliency within me, and use those skills I'd learned over the years of solution-finding instead of dwelling in stress? Absolutely. I've found that mindset is everything, and even in those moments of feeling on the brink of burnout, it's that final chip of the pick-axe that uncovers the gold you've been working for all along.

It wasn't until the end of the event, the launch that brought that first book to the world, where it all soaked in. I was giving the final speech of the night and, after I wrapped it up, all the authors gathered on stage—15 women and one man who had given their all in sharing their stories of empowerment and success—and the audience gave us a standing ovation. Flowers were given, the last of the books were autographed and I felt a sense that we changed a lot of lives that day. It was such an incredible event, and I couldn't wait to get started on *Empowering Women to Succeed Volume 2: From Burnout to Victory*.

THE LITTLE BURNOUTS: LESSONS OF LIFE THAT BRING US SUCCESS!

Randi Goodman

My whole life has been a series of small burnouts that have led to big victories. I ran ragged for years, therapy after therapy for my kids, all of who were challenged with learning disabilities, trying to give them the most support to be the best they can be. I worked tirelessly to help them know they can learn to overcome any challenge and have the tools and knowledge to deal with any situation.

I was running a household, taking care of the bills and financials, supporting the schools so they could properly support my children, running charity events and turning them into huge community fun fairs. A lot of my time was spent sitting on committees, being Chair of school council, becoming a second Dan in Karate, bearing and raising four boys, keeping my mind in business, being a mom, a wife, a daughter, a sister and a friend; then came the ultimate success at hosting business events including trade shows, conferences, workshops, courses, podcasts, reverse marketing, becoming title author of a #1 International Bestselling Series, and so much more. Burnt out, you ask?

You can say I was leaning in that direction. For some of the things, I can say that, yes, I got burnt out. Burnt out of doing everything on my own, most of the time, burnt out of being in the schools and giving all my free time to them, burnt out or on the cusp of it in challenges with my marriage, and burnt out in working towards business goals and not being able to achieve them. So yes, for those endeavours, I can say I was burnt out.

My days are busy, whether it's with kids, business, taking care of the house, or something else. That need to take care of my own health and wellness becomes more immanent every day. I feel the aches and pains in my body; I need to be conscious to make sure I am in a position to function for my kids and I. When I slow down, listen to my body and mind, and make sure I tend to them so my immune system doesn't drop, I retain the strength to keep going, to do that which drives me every day, and achieve my goals.

We get burnt out, but we don't see the signs that are right in front of our face. We also tend to give and give to the point of exhaustion. I know in my life, I have given and given; but the funny thing is that people don't always, or often, give back. They don't even think to invite you. They are happy to receive, but not so happy to give. Giving can be exhausting, after the fact. What does that mean? When you give, it is the most wonderful thing. Give without expectation, give without desiring something in return. It will come back to you, even if not directly. What I add here is that sometimes we notice, after a very long time, that through all the giving we never saw much in return and that can bring us down or even cause us to be regretful of the giving, to deter us from giving in the future. How do we get beyond this burnout, this exhaustion of giving ourselves away? We need to be in control of our own mindset, take control over ourselves, learn to look from another point of view, and not have expectations that diminish our giving nature.

I have always done what felt right to me, and that's been an important step in being able to give without expectation, and to set the path for my own and others' greatest success. For example, I never was one for religion, hence I stopped going to synagogue when I was a teenager. I didn't see the point. Everybody would sit and talk while the Rabbi was talking, the elders would shush the younger people, but they never listened anyway. I was bored and stopped going, but that didn't mean there wasn't something to celebrate or something to believe in; it just meant I didn't have an appreciation for the religious part.

There's a funny, and not-so-funny, story. When I got engaged to be married, my husband-to-be's father insisted that we join the family for Erev Yom Kippur to hear the blowing of the shofar. In the Jewish religion, you attend synagogue the night before Yom Kippur after having a large dinner before the full-day fast; this signifies the New Moon and calls people together. So at 21, I had to go back to synagogue on this one night of the year. It was something I was giving to my future husband, something I was giving to his father, and let me tell you, I really felt it was torture to me. Nonetheless, I went. In attending this night for the next couple of years, I really could not handle it anymore. The synagogue had two floors, most of the congregation sat on the main level while the upper level outlined the perimeter of the room on three sides, maybe five rows in total. The windows had beautiful stained glass designs, but the main congregation area was insignificant otherwise. I never really listened to what was going on and any chance I could I would leave the room or chat with my sister-in-law. One fine day, we were at synagogue while I was pregnant with my first son, and my husband and I saw the Rabbi reading a People magazine, which was on his podium. That was the final straw. I had never seen this in any other synagogue, and I decided enough was enough. We got up in the middle of service, announced to those we were with that we would never be back, and left.

It wasn't just that experience in synagogue though. I used to believe in reincarnation when I was a kid. I believed in spirits, I even believed in haunted houses. I had a friend in kindergarten who lived across the street from the school and he believed that his house was haunted, so we used to have a lot of fun with that. So I did believe spirits were out there and I believed something was up there, I just didn't believe there was a G-d. If I couldn't see him or her, then how could it be? (I guess you could say the same about spirits!)

I do love the stories; I love what they represent, but not the part about the need to believe in something other than yourself. I truly believe we need to believe in ourselves to trust ourselves, to trust our instincts, to know that we are making the right decisions. This might have been the route to my thinking today. This might not resonate for you, and that's ok if it doesn't. I don't judge people; you can believe in whatever you wish to, if it makes you happy, empowers you, and allows you to live with great morals and ethics. It empowers me to know that I believe in *me.* I have friends who believe in a multitude of things; I appreciate them and their views, whether I believe them myself or not. We have so much to learn from other religions, cultures and beliefs. When we expand on our own beliefs and thoughts, that is how we grow and it's how we get and do better in this world. This is how we help many! Belief is about taking action for me, regardless of what you believe. This has empowered me immensely and given me the ability to help so many people throughout my life.

When I was growing up, I made others happy by doing things I really didn't like, which made me miserable. I gave my power away, didn't stick up for my own beliefs in some situations and that made me terribly uncomfortable. I ended up doing it again when I started to date my now-ex. I gave my power away again. I had to take it back! I had to do what I wanted and not live doing what other people wanted or expected of me. The story doesn't end there.

Learning how to take my power back, and having the courage to believe in myself and do things in a way that work for me, is something I cultivated and developed over the years from many experiences and many different people. She has passed now, but when my Boobie Sally (grandmother in Jewish), my mom's mom, was alive, I used to spend every day with her after my first son Joey was born. My mom's side had survived the Holocaust and all the tragedy that came with that, so my Boobie would tell me stories sometimes. Hearing those stories from her inspired me, shook me, and made me believe that you can overcome any obstacle. She was the true definition of "burnout to victory." Having to endure one of the worst times in human history, giving up on your faith in G-d, but still pushing forward to create a happy life, was very motivating to me. I remember one time getting into a conversation about G-d. I always thought she believed in G-d because she said "thank G-d" as a comment to events in life, until she told me, "how could there be a G-d? If there was one, how could it allow this to happen?" My Boobie was burnt out from believing in a higher power.

Ok, enough of universe, spirit, energy and G-d...

The little burnouts come in many different ways, but can lead to the biggest victories in ways we might not expect. In the first volume of this series, I mentioned that I took piano lessons; I did from three years old until I was 15, when my mom finally allowed me to quit. At the time I hated piano, probably because they made me cut my nails off and I had to practice for an hour every day. All I wanted to do was play and do my own thing! I was totally burnt out from piano lessons, having to practice every day and not do the things I wanted to do. I wanted to socialize, party, be with my friends, and not be stuck in front of the piano.

I had absolutely no control over the fact that I had to take piano and practice for one hour every day. I bring it up because it made a huge impact directly on what I do today. Today I speak on stage to crowds of thousands, all across North America. During piano recitals, I used to completely blank out. We would have to present our Royal Conservatory music in front of all of our parents, friends and the other students. We did not use books, notes or anything in front of us while presenting; it all had to be from memory. It was terrifying. You know, they say that people fear presenting in front of others more than they fear death itself, so you can feel a little bit of what I was experiencing at the time. Well, there were a few times that this happened. What, you ask? I totally blanked out. Yep, that's right, totally blanked out, couldn't remember where I was in the song, what the last note was or the next one. They had to bring the book out for me to continue presenting. It was embarrassing and, for those that know me, I don't get embarrassed!

Even though I speak on stages all around the world, it took me a while to get over my stage fright. It was only a few years ago, in 2010 or 2011, when I would ask whoever was helping me at an event to make an announcement on the microphone from a back corner where no one could see us. I wouldn't even do that! Look at me now!

So how did I do it? It was a challenge I needed to overcome in order to succeed. When I got into doing events, it was inevitable that I would have to speak on stage to people, whether to introduce my speakers, say hello to the audience and welcome them, thank them for being with us—whatever it was, I would have to be up there at some point. So I decided that since I have absolutely no issue talking in a crowd, in a meeting or one on one, for business or pleasure, then when I am on stage, I would do the same. I would just imagine I am talking to my buddies, focus on one person or one spot in the room and all my nervousness should go away, right? It helped a lot, let me tell you. I still felt a tad bit nervous prior to going on stage, my heart racing, but eventually I felt comfortable with that calming thought in my head. See your audience as equals, you can even practice on stage without anyone in the room to get comfortable standing and presenting, or ask family members and friends to listen to you so you can practice.

I got my power back and it became a big victory, speaking on stages around the world. I did it by using whatever tools I had to give myself to have the courage to do better, become stronger, succeed and overcome my fears. One of the strongest things I learned was to stop internalizing my feelings of fear on stage and instead focus on being of service. I make it my priority to give without expectation, to give as much as possible while on stage, inspiring and informing those in the audience to learn what they need to succeed. Every time I do that, my fear dissipates, and my presentation gets better and is really well-received. I know because of those words people say afterwards, thank you, and the sense I get of having truly been of service.

It becomes fun on stage, too, just by giving from my heart, having a conversation and interacting with my audience. Getting down from the stage, truly connecting in a way that feels good, bringing people up to the stage or having them talk with one another—these are just some of the things that changed my fearful experiences to fun ones, and ones that give and support.

Learning from the best is vital to success and overcoming too, so I took courses from the most incredible mentors. James Dentley in Chicago, who has an established track record of teaching the best of the best to speak and sell from stages all over the world, and Gordon So in Toronto, who has been speaking on stage internationally for over 20 years and knows exactly how to engage, educate and motivate his audience—these are the kinds of leaders I surround myself with to take life's moments of mini-burnouts and turn them into great victories.

It's because of challenging myself on so many levels that I've stepped from burnout to victory. One of the things I have always felt strongly about, no matter what I was doing, is giving to those in need. I am always bringing in charities to support at my events, whether it's A Celebration of Women™ Foundation or Million Dollar Smiles; they are always included. I have a strong belief in giving others tools and resources to be successful, to surpass the challenges we all face in our lives. Some of us are lucky to be in situations where we have more support or finances to give, but many are not in the same place, so it is our duty, our gift, to be able to support any way we can. I have felt this way since I was a young child.

This takes me way back to being a kid again. I have no idea what drew me to it but I volunteered for the Leukemia charity. No one in my family had it but for some reason I wanted to volunteer. I later went on to volunteer for many organizations like the UJA Walk, Variety Village, Hadassah Bazaar, Hadassah Wizo, year of galas for YRAP, A

Celebration of Women™ Foundation, Million Dollar Smiles and so many more!

When my children were in school I was lucky to be able to volunteer there too, in the classroom, on school trips, chairing the BBQ committee and sitting on school council in one school and being chair at school council in another—yes, I like to give a lot. At times, my kids were in three different schools at the same time, so it did get busy. We had incredible events at the school and I ran them for years. The feeling I received from giving back to my community was so valuable. Besides my kids, the one thing that made me feel great was doing all this volunteer work and knowing I was helping someone. This is a huge passion of mine, and something I include in every aspect of my business today.

It's important though to always remember: don't get swept up in the giving, and forget about yourself. It's a fine balance, and if you're not at your best—your healthiest, most optimum state—you are not able to give to anyone else. I've had to learn that as I grow from those little burnouts to the victories in all that I do.

Even though I spent a lot of my time giving, I had a really hard time saying 'thank you' from people when they gave me a compliment. I always remember my mom telling me, after someone gives me a compliment, *'say thank you!'* Would you believe that I had such a hard time getting those words to come out of my mouth? I also had a hard time accepting things from others. I guess I didn't value *me* enough. I needed to grow to a place where I would be empowered, but that did not come so quickly.

Volunteering led not only to my love of business, but also to my love of organizing and planning events. It was only natural that these two merged at some point, which is when I started to do business trade shows, B2Bs (business to business) where we had 50 or more exhibitors, three or more speakers and hundreds of attendees to mingle with in a beautiful setting of a banquet hall. In one room, energy soaring, people chatting and business being conducted. It enthralled me. People loved to attend and network with vendors and each other, which soon led to having speakers on stage to present and share information as well. A few years later, my business partner Gordon So and I continued on to create business conferences where the focus was on the speaker and not so much on the vendor, allowing us to provide maximum information to the audience to help them improve their personal and professional lives. I can't express how rewarding it is to know you have changed someone's life for the better!

I had always had help from people, including a handful of volunteers for each event, but I had never actually built a 'team.' When I met Gordon, we met in a coffee shop with no plan and no idea what would transpire. We knew there was a dream, excitement in the conversation, and a goal going forward. There was no plan of dates, but that conversation between two people who took action, in sync, with the same purpose, evolved into the incredible four large events (and counting) we have today, and the many smaller ones and courses we teach hands on. It was an evolution, a direction, that led to where it is today and will continue to grow to greater things. Build your team and allow things to take place, allow the flow, trust it, go with it—what transpires will surprise you. The belief and action taken for something greater and more rewarding does lead to success. We now have a surrounding of incredible people who we work with and support on a regular basis. I am so grateful and proud to call them my team.

In 2011, one of those large events, the Toronto Women's Expo, began. I had been doing business events for two years already, but when introduced to Rhonda Shulman, we hit it off and went full force with our first event under this name. We had a blast, made a little bit of money, and I decided that it needed to continue, so with the support of my friend, I continued on solo.

As mentioned in the first book, I held my first and only to date, two-day expo in Toronto at Downsview Park, December 2012. Although the results were devastating, despite the efforts and money that went into marketing and promoting, I couldn't allow that to deter me from my goals. I was burnt out, exhausted, beaten down. I did pull back from having a large event the next calendar year and worked on building relationships and seminars with smaller groups with my good friend Catherine Anne Clark, founder of A Celebration of Women™ Foundation. I was terrified to host another expo or trade show, regardless of the fact that the previous ones were great successes. It was really difficult for me to trust that it could be successful again—I was scared out of my mind!

By the end of the summer of 2013, something clicked. Something inside me had more of a desire to produce another trade show. I made a conscious decision that I would be investing in my own personal growth, with time and money, and plan my next Toronto Women's Expo in January of 2014. There was a victory in stepping forward and going for it. Being an entrepreneur really means being resilient, in the true sense of the word. Entrepreneurs go through ups and downs, whether it's financially or mentally. It takes great strength to see it through and carry your goals and dreams to fruition. I had to be willing to fall flat on my face, and I did that. I was juggling four kids, a separation, trying to find myself in my personal and business life, all the while trying to grow a business. I truly believe my willingness to stand up after a fall is what opened the doors for more positive to come into my life. This is where Gordon So came in.

After meeting with Gordon in the fall of 2013, my business flourished. Incredible speakers stormed the stage at my events, I started podcasting, book writing and blogging, teaching live and online courses. That is just the start, who knows where the future will take us. Thank you Gordon! You are a rock, a creative genius, a connecting wizard, and a great friend.

I would not be where I am today though without learning some hard lessons and overcoming obstacles I had been facing since I was a kid. Along with learning to overcome my fear of presenting in public, I also had to learn to say no. I had always had trouble saying no. Have you ever felt that way? I remember when I hired a business coach back in 2010, Mike Bradford, Business Coach Toronto. One of the biggest things he instilled in me at the time was to say *no!* I had such a hard time saying no to people, to my detriment. For those that study, read, or attend learning sessions about professional growth, you know that you need to spend your time on things that produce for you. If you are spending a lot of time doing projects that don't create income or lead to it, then you are most likely wasting your time. I know that I have spent a lot of time on professional projects that never resulted in any income, and I am not talking about charities. All of those projects led to the detriment of my family and my home. Being a single mom, I have four kids that I need to support, so I can't be spending all my time not earning.

I remember one of the hardest days I ever had. I had to say no to someone I respected very much in the business world. We had collaborated and supported one another for a while and I had no intention of not continuing to do so. He proposed an opportunity to me that we had met on a couple of times, discussed some details, but when it came right down to it, there was not going to be any money to be made. I had a really tough decision to make. My instinctive answer was to say *yes!* When I discussed this with my coach at the time, he said, "how can you take this on when you are not earning money in what you are doing now? You need to spend time on your business and figure out how to generate income from that instead of taking on more things that don't earn."

I have to tell you this hit me at my core. It was not easy to take but I totally agreed with him; I just couldn't figure out how to tell this wonderful person that I would not be able to do it. I had to take the financial figures and go by that and just explain that it was one of the most difficult decisions I had to make. I explained that I could not do it for financial reasons, but I would support and promote as I always had, even help get some vendors, but I could not partner with this venture. He was so sweet, as I always knew he was, and totally understood and agreed.

Although this was extremely difficult for me, having a coach to help me through and validate the decision not to participate, was extremely powerful and empowered me like never before. I was on a mission to succeed and having someone to help me through was the best thing for me and my business. I have used coaches and mentors for many things and will always continue to do so. We need influential people around us, those that lift us up and not bring us down. Look around you and see who the closest people are to you. How do they make you feel; happy, sad, elated, invigorated, or do they put you down, make you feel terrible about yourself or even like crap? I challenge you to take a look right now. Write the name of someone who is close to you, who you spend a lot of time with, then write down how you feel when you just wrote down their name. Do that for each person in your life that you spend time with, whether family, friends or business-related. Now that you have that in front of you, you can analyze whether you are spending too much time with those people or not. Now I want you to write down all the positive people you can think of, whether you spend a lot of time with them or no time with them. If there are too many negative ones, replace a lot of that time with the positive ones you wrote down. Start replacing negative with positive. You may not be able to remove all of the toxic people but you can make sure most of your time is enjoyed with people that lift you up and whom you can lift up!

I choose the people who lift me up, and it has made all the difference. Another opportunity appeared to me later on with Scott Paton and Gordon. Scott is a very motivating and successful business owner who has been podcasting since 2005. His first podcast reached 375,000 subscribers in the first year! When he asked me to create an e-course with him, I made sure it was well planned out, and allowed both of us to make money on it. What we ended up creating was a course about publishing books and how to properly market them. In the first hour, it had already reached 100 students and a few hours later it hit 500! When I woke up the next day I saw it had 2,000 students enrolled. Because we had a solid plan and marketed correctly, our joint venture became an overnight hit. The best part about this project is that it doesn't burn me out. The process in making the course took a while, but it was fun because I got to use my skills and experiences to help create it. Now that it is successful, I don't have to keep worrying about it taking up the time I use to take care of myself.

You need to value yourself no matter what, and across all elements of life. Making the choices that are best for you, while still giving back, allows you to do that. Ignoring yourself, helping others to a fault, taking care of someone else and putting them first, only harms yourself and your family. You need to value your own abilities. There are people around you that, no matter how much you do for them, feel it's never enough; there are people around you that expect too much from you and you can never live up to it. I've learned it's okay to say no, and to let those experiences go.

It's also important to monetize your business and not just help others in the process, just as I learned and made changes towards all those years ago. There's mental income you receive in giving, but in business let's be honest here, it doesn't put food on the table nor a roof over your family's head, nor does it pay the bills. Connecting with others and building a team around you of people who elevate you, people who fill in the gaps so you don't waste time on things you are not strong or good at, leads you in a positive money flow direction and helps a lot of people at the same time.

Finding balance in your life is the key to overcoming the burnouts that creep up on us. The most important thing is the shift in mindset. I want everyone to know they are capable, worthy and valued, even if not from those they seek it from, but from those that will give from a true place of care and service. When we learn to focus on what makes us happy and who makes us happy, things become a lot easier. Do the things you love, help others, practice self-care, and don't let anyone take you for granted! We all have a spark in us, one that can't be denied; live your purpose, and your mini-burnouts can become the biggest victories.

JOURNEY TO LOVE

Lisa Bartello

On the regular I sit on the floor in the round white room with walnut-stained floors and glass windows that are three stories high. This room is total serenity for me. The place where I guide meditation that sometimes I could swear I feel pure love. The white light and the sunshine are always dominant no matter what the weather. It's almost total glass and full-length, three-storey high windows to keep the light shining. The roundness of the room gives me that feeling like I am safe and enveloped by the light. There's something very special I have experienced in this place that is almost indescribable. I've had people bare their souls in here. People bawling their eyes out; taking a sacred piece of themselves, and sharing. People grinning from ear to ear like, 'I get it – I really get it.' People who twist up their face in such a way that I knew they were far out of their comfort zone and struggling. People looking at me with a soul connection that requires no words. People connecting their eyes to mine as I sit on the floor and thanking me in such a manner that I could never forget them. People I know I have made an unforgettable impression on, hoping they know I was just the conduit for their own growth, evolution and journey toward love. Each time I start out with the same question: how do you honour yourself?

This question of how we honour ourselves reflects back to me often, sometimes hitting me right in the face. Such simple laws of attraction that tell me when I love myself my life is full, the energy is lighter, the world is often euphoric, my vibration is magnetic and I don't feel resistance like I am at battle with myself every second of every single day. Yet I shudder to think just how long it has taken me to get to this place. Every single thing I have guided in that meditation room has been a reflection of where I was both refusing and longing to go for what seemed like an eternity.

I realize now that by not loving myself and wanting to be all the things I wasn't, I attracted the experiences in my life that would validate the exact same lack and unloving thoughts about my truth that I tried so desperately not to embody. In every step of my journey I was reminded of everything that I believed I wasn't. When you don't love yourself, quite simply, you reflect and mirror that experience constantly back through your relationships in order to amplify your wounds. It's the perfect storm.

The journey of life is such that we have to constantly touch our wounds in order to learn. It's the ultimate dichotomy; we get the experiences before the lessons. Suffering creates the driving force. Up to now the driving forces in my life that were the impetus for change have often been my children—up until recently I couldn't remember a time when I was loving and honouring myself enough to make me and what I desired the driving force. As I've shifted my quest to make the driving force myself, I think the catalyst was a series of synchronistic events.

The universe always presents clues for our higher learning. One such clue was when a friend who is an elite coach and mentor offered to mentor my son for free, but my son refused. I was so astonished that my son would so carelessly bypass such an opportunity. I ended up in the course my son was invited to and I realized by the end that the learning opportunity was indeed meant for me. My friend looked at me and said that the very best thing I could offer anyone was to work on myself; 'Lisa, work on yourself.' Vivid moments of clarity where I realized love and light is solely an inside job.

There was also a shift toward intimate love as well. The only logical place to start was with me. It's the inherent knowing that everything we want and long for can only be delivered through loving ourselves first and foremost—love is literally the window to everything magic—and I refuse to live a life where I'm too scared to feel. I refuse to repeat the patterns of my previous relationships. Proof that I've grown and I don't need to repeat the lessons of my past. "Love is always the final and complete cure to our inner demons," the quote from Brendon Burchard eternally etched in my brain. Truth.

My residing belief is that the partner I attract is a reflection of my ultimate whole, self-love.

I'm constantly reminding others: you don't get who you want, you get who you are. Am I courageous enough to change the paradigm I've lived by? "You expect the love you think you deserve." My favourite quote from the movie, *Perks of Being A Wallflower*. "Yes indeed I am courageous enough." My journey has set the tone for both my future relationships and what has become a burning life purpose as a healer, and a teacher.

Where to start? I want you to read this so that it feels like it's torture. As if it feels like the mania was so endless that it's almost unfathomable. The mania started with my body. I spent many years yo-yo dieting, starving myself, trying every weight loss program available, binging and purging. I went to bed countless nights punishing myself for the food misdeeds of the day—such a torturous cycle—the cycle of shame, guilt and punishment with the vow to do better the next day. I will never attempt to multiply the days, weeks and years that I lived that cycle—quantifying it would kill me. Such a bitter cycle that nothing positive could ever truly evolve from.

As a young child I was always super skinny. I used to refer to myself as 'Ethiopian,' which is abhorrent, in retrospect, feeling it was acceptable to compare my body to starving children. Ignorance was always bliss. My coaches at swimming and my family doctor would ask my parents why they didn't feed me. I was skinny and I could eat like a house on fire. Pure sugar was my favourite food group. Later I would learn that my cravings for sugar represented emotional imbalances all my life, but back then it was very black and white—I liked 'bad food.' At some stage my parents followed the advice of doctors and coaches and put me on a special diet to gain weight. Yes, you read that correctly, *gain* weight.

We all have our growing and learning challenges. I know this now, but then I felt I had been given much greater challenges than my fair share. I had no gratitude for the gifts I had received. Concepts like gratitude were so foreign. I used to refer to myself as a misfit. Buckteeth that were severely damaged from the days of tetracycline, braces, coke bottle bottom glasses, mammoth curly hair and awkwardly tall. I literally used to think if only I had been 5'8" instead of 5'10" my life would be better. Yes, it came down to two inches—as if two inches could ever encapsulate the person that I am. For someone who always wanted to shrink and be less than, I wasn't exactly given the physical stature or the personality to match. Every lesson came at me from the opposing. The Yin and the Yang. I tried to be less than, more introvert, quiet, un-opinionated and dispassionate, and I longed to be physically and characteristically small. The truth at the core of who I am is exactly the opposite—I fought so hard against this. Ironically, on the exterior, people believed I was the picture of self-confidence. I was masterful at hiding my truth. It's so painful for me to even type such stupidity now. I was attracting all those soul lessons into my life that would teach me that if I didn't love myself from the start I would surely learn in the end.

At a certain point I started naturally gaining weight like every teenager does. I didn't understand I was growing like a normal human being. I had my own ideas about how I would deal. What I remember most about the fad diets is starving. Wondering what was wrong with me and why I had so little self-control. Not realizing that I needed the subsistence for basic survival. Sitting in French class my stomach would growl so loud that my best friend who sat behind me would inevitably start laughing. We would both get in trouble. Perhaps I could've seen the signs then that this wasn't the best approach? Nope....

The next chapter was the bulimia years. I'd throw up and go to the gym almost daily and work out doing high impact aerobics for at least an hour. Health nut... I remember the owner of the gym approaching me and remarking how much weight I'd lost and when I told her I wanted to lose more I remember the look on her face—total knowing. I'll never forget the way she looked at me. It was almost as if she was imploring me to listen with her eyes explaining I was already quite thin (of course in retrospect I was terribly skinny). It was as if her stomach was knotted witnessing my eating disorder and hoping her inputs might get me to open my eyes to the body dysmorphia. Among my most uncomfortable memories from those years is babysitting.

I'd rummage through the cupboards and look for food, trying to find the less obvious choices so it wouldn't show that I was actually attempting to eat them out of house and home. Then I would throw up. I knew when they came home they would know. That feeling of shame and guilt and embarrassment would only amplify my feelings of self-loathing. When it comes to addiction or any type of unworthiness we all try to hide. As I write this I realize I have never confessed these memories to anyone.

I propelled forward with all these varied experiences with my weight and had the matching vocabulary to go with my distorted body image. I used the word 'fat' to describe myself almost more than I took breaths. I often wonder when the self-hatred became palpable? In university I went to see my family doctor and told her I didn't like my weight and, "oh by the way – I was bulimic in high school." I shudder to think just how skinny I actually was. There was never any emotional connection with my family doctor growing up. In her cold, disconnected manner she referred me to a psychiatrist.

I have appointments along my journey where I was a seeker—always looking for external validation—memories that fall in my filing cabinet of life under 'things that were a total waste of time,' and these visits are definitely filed there. I remember this man I perceived to be wealthy from his prescription pad and his matching Jaguar parked outside. He didn't assess me at all in terms of my environment. He didn't ask me what was going on in my life. My dad had just recently been diagnosed with cancer at the tender age of 45. You'd think that might have been relevant or perhaps at least impacting my state of mind? Ironically I was majoring in Sociology, the study of human behaviour, and I so desperately wanted someone to get in my mind with me and understand my human behaviour.

Clearly we are all meant to awaken and discover our own evolution at some point. I was still very much classifying this seeking under 'concepts lost on me.' Seriously, where was my inner voice back then? Nonexistent. I remember the psychiatrist asking me to turn around and show him my body and subsequently writing me a prescription for Prozac. When I told him I didn't want it he said, "vhy? All the vomen vant it." I can still hear the words clearly echoing in my head. I went a few more times and literally had a small stack of prescriptions for Prozac. Prozac was his purported solution to my weight. I filled the first one—took them one day feeling horrible and disoriented, so much so I don't think I've ever been able to take anti-depressants again. Miraculously I was able to find other ways of becoming emotionally numb without antidepressants—but make no mistake we all have to deal with things eventually. This man actually told me Prozac would help me lose weight, both sad and scary but I was only 19 and shrugged it off with a joke. I didn't begin to comprehend the severity. Today if someone tried to diagnose me in that manner I would rip them a new asshole. There was nothing in my line of sight that was showing me the importance of simple self-love.

Like everything else in life, when you don't embrace and love yourself the universe will find a way to put harder and harsher lessons in your path. Enter the pregnancy years. If I thought I had body image issues before having children, getting pregnant would ultimately show me much deeper mental and physical trials and anguish. I truly think this is one of the hardest psychological and physical journeys women go through. As women we are given the gift of life and the gift of procreation over our male counterparts. This is truly one of the most precious gifts on earth. It's the only time souls are unified in our entire lives. I think over time, many of us have lost sight of how truly priceless this gift is. There is no place for regrets in life, only learning, but being pregnant is certainly a demarcation point I revisit to come to terms with the self-loathing. I couldn't just allow my body to grow that life inside me. I have such a connection with children. As a soul I know I'm an eternal mother and the only clear purpose I've ever known to my absolute core is that of being a mother. I see babies for the true miracle of life that they are. In spite of this I despised what pregnancy did to my body. I have the rest of my life to live with that, cognizant of the fact that I carried my beautiful children for nine months each without ever having looked in the mirror at my naked body with love for the miracle of life inside me. I just wanted the miracle without the nine months. The Yin without the Yang. I remember going to the doctor, pregnant with my first son, and regularly getting weighed. In the final few weeks I triumphantly declared, 'no fucking way would I weigh in anymore.' Even in those critical moments I reduced myself to a number. Every. Single. Day.

Life is summed up in a series of lessons within each and every chapter. Having children brought a new chapter in self-loathing while in parallel an equally fierce love for my children—a love so intense that I didn't even know I was capable of a love like that. I had all these stretch marks on my skin. My body would never be the same. Prior to that I always anticipated that some magical potion, lotion, diet and sustained 'willpower' would finally result in the perfection I was so desperately seeking. I was so naïve, not realizing I was already perfection. I wasn't prepared for the physical changes. I had already defined myself as a number but these changes were much more devastating. I desperately needed someone to tell me I was beautiful and I never understood I had to tell myself. I truly think it was the universe saying to me, 'ok you didn't like yourself before then you need a bigger test.' Those harder and harsher lessons until we learn. As Oprah says, "we get the whispers in life and when we don't listen eventually we get the brick." Then of course I had these new little miracles of life that I tried to validate myself through—I could pour all my love that I was desperately seeking for myself into them. Transference. What I wanted and needed most could be replicated through me to my kids. I could love my children so powerfully as the greatest gifts from God but then somehow not love myself? Crazy. I couldn't see the imbalance.

I spent almost two more decades with this self-loathing. Abhorring my body, yo-yo dieting, being less than, shrinking away from myself. Let me tell you, the look inward was harsh to say the least.

Turning points. I am queued by a conversation with my sister who recently had her second baby. My confident, beautiful sister. An elite athlete. Swimming team captain two years in a row at UCLA. I have always felt she held the world at her fingertips. In a weaker moment of intense exhaustion, illness and sleep deprivation without having slept for days, she told me how ugly she felt. How unattractive. She's never been a superficial person. She loves her babies to her core. She is also cognizant of the fact she has great character and has always been able to acknowledge her gifts….but….still….this. I had nothing to offer.

I could feel the struggle I had felt for an eternity through her words. Then magically her son fell asleep in her arms while we were talking. It was as if it was a sign from God. The baby who rarely slept, fell asleep on her, so innocent, beautiful and perfect. I took her picture. It was magical. I could literally feel her intense beauty. As a mother. As a woman. As a warrior. As a goddess. I got up the next day and literally wept looking at this picture. I was catapulted into memories. How could I have allowed anything physical in this lifetime to ever define me? It's through this lens the world shifted around me. That lens that was so utterly shattered. Where was that lens so long ago?

Looking back through the rearview mirror I wonder what was the ultimate catalyst for change? The thought of my children not loving themselves? There's that driving force again. Was it a reflection of life as their role model that I wasn't living up to my highest self? My truth? There was also fear of repeating mistakes and relationships of the past that were mirrored in my self-loathing. In order to prove I had learned the lessons of the past I needed to love myself. Period. Regardless, I'm grateful I perceived any lack of self-love in my children or myself as my fault and my responsibility. I woke up one day and realized if I didn't love myself, my children would grow with an image of a mother that was never truly happy—never having truly lived. This was not going to be my story. Finally an innate understanding that life was meant for living and loving and I was wasting precious time.

I remember lying down in bed one night and just going to sleep. No punishment. In the morning I remember feeling different. My inner dialogue wasn't torture anymore. Surrender. Who knew I could just surrender with acceptance and it would give me peace? I would look in the mirror naked, at the parts I had never loved and I would express my love. I looked in the mirror and rewrote the story. The story was fiction in the beginning but in the end it became nonfiction.

I discovered this layer that needed to be undressed for the first time. A soul longing for love. Then magically, it happens. Suddenly. Unexpectedly. I took a different approach to dirty words like 'fat' and 'diet' and decided to exercise without expectation. I never weigh myself anymore. I was never the number on the scale.

This journey of self-love has brought me magic. It has afforded me knowledge. I could never be defined as a number. I am energy. I am vibration. I am frequency. I have literally transformed and activated my DNA. When we love ourselves we literally start to experience ascension. Every single second of every single day the billions of cells in my body are no longer in resistance. The energy required not to love and honour myself was both exhausting and damaging in every aspect. I look in the mirror now and see a person who is able to love openly, compassionately and unapologetically. I see a mother who can truly love her children in a way I couldn't before—unconditionally. Love truly heals. I see a beautiful woman, although this took more time. I softened the story until I could look deep within, knowing at the very core of my being that I am and always was perfect. I am eternal love.

I have been told time and again that my love is extremely powerful; powerful enough to heal and I realize triumphantly that this journey to self-love is my gift. My vocation. This journey has propelled me into my life purpose; teaching about the power of love and the energy of love. Love has literally been the window to my third eye, my intuition and my inner voice. Suddenly there is such a clear channel.

Alongside my lifelong passion as a Realtor and Real Estate Investor, I can finally embrace that I am a healer and a teacher and my burning life purpose comes from serving others. I could never do the intuitive counselling, readings, healing, guiding meditation and energy work that I do now without having gone down this path. I embrace the lessons and the journey that has become my gift to the world. My gifts come in the form of words. Words heal. Love is quite simply transformative, both emotionally and physically. Love transcends anything and everything; mind, body and spirit. Being in a true state of self-love makes us whole and when we are whole we vibrate at a much higher frequency. It is that frequency that makes us contagious—I was never a number on the scale. Ultimately when we are whole we can truly love exponentially and unconditionally, which has been my unwitting quest. I often bow deeply in gratitude for this journey and the decades of lack inside me that could deliver me to here, to my true life purpose.

With respect to intimate relationships I have no doubt that my life includes a great love story. It's inevitable. It's part of my soul's journey. Without a doubt, one day I will write a bestseller on love and relationships. In all my relationships I can offer abundant love and compassion because it resides inside me. As Einstein said, "energy cannot be created or destroyed, it can only be changed from one form to another." That is truly the energy and power of love—it changes its composition as it becomes whole. It becomes an undeniable law of attraction.

The simple law is love. With this metamorphosis, finally the courage to receive love. Our ability to receive love is directly proportionate only to the degree of love we have for ourselves. I will have a partner who loves me as deeply as I have the courage to love myself. I spent years seeking external validation when none could have ever been found in all eternity. And with this love I am healed. Love is truly the beginning, the end and everything in between.

.

KNOCK KNOCK, WHO'S THERE? YOUR WAKE UP CALL

Ellie Savoy

It was a gorgeous summer afternoon on June 8th, 2008. Perfect weather for hosting a public open house for one of my real estate listings. A few people had shown up to explore this lovely property set back from the road that sat high on a knoll in a private setting. I had some downtime so I decided to check my landline for messages. I looked at my watch. It was around 3:30 p.m.

I dialed in and had one message waiting. I never thought in a million years that I would ever receive a message like this. It was my brother telling me that my mother had passed away in the hospital that day. Granted my mother had been ill for eight years and she was declining. I had a feeling that the time was drawing closer, but hearing that she was gone was such a shock. It was so final. There was no way to change it. My brother was in shock too and wasn't thinking straight when he left me the message. As I began to absorb what I was listening to, I felt my heart racing. I started to cry. I felt like I was going to have a panic attack. I felt fragile.

My mind seemed to be going a hundred miles an hour with so many thoughts rushing through it. What would happen to my dad after being with my mother for over 50 years? He had been an amazing caregiver for the past eight years, and it became his life day in and day out. His kids were far away living overseas. I called my husband to tell him the news. He told me he was coming to get me and not to drive home because I was dealing with shock. I told him I would be alright. I packed up my things, turned off the lights, locked the door, called the homeowner and headed home.

When I got home I called my dad. My heart felt broken. I felt so bad for him. I realized that he was the one affected the most by all of this. His lifelong partner was gone and he was alone for the first time in his life at 70 years old.

I made the trip back home to England to be with my family. Seeing my dad for the first time in this new situation was heartbreaking. I can still see it and feel it like it was yesterday. My mother's slippers were by the stool in the kitchen. Her walking stick was hooked over the back of the stool. Her eyeglass case was on the kitchen countertop. My dad tried to be strong for all of us but seeing him grieving was one of the toughest times in my life.

My brother and sister arrived home before me. They had already started to embrace the reality and had been to the funeral home. I chatted with them about their experience. They were glad they went but they said it was very difficult. I felt like I was in such a dilemma. I wanted to go but I was afraid. I told my dad how I felt. He said it was up to me, but to make sure I didn't regret my decision. After all, I wouldn't have a second chance. He was right. It was then or never. I dug deep inside myself and made the decision to go. My husband was also with both of us. I remember entering the funeral home, and before I knew it we were inside the room where she was. It was so sudden and I didn't have a chance to compose myself.

She didn't look peaceful at all. I realized my back was up against the wall as if I was trying to escape being in the room. My breathing was heavy and fast. I was so overwhelmed. I had never experienced the death of a close family member before. I always showed compassion for others who were dealing with death, but suddenly I was dealing with it firsthand. For some reason in that room I remembered the saying, "you can't take it with you when you die." My mother was so consumed with her home and garden. She loved spending time taking care of both and having my dad decorate every year. It seemed to be so important to her and almost an obsession, yet none of it was going with her. Why was I striving so hard to have more material things at the expense of my own well-being just to leave it all behind one day? Something about it really got my attention.

I was often working six or seven days a week. It seemed normal to me, yet I was neglecting my own needs. I had a pattern of working until I was exhausted and would only take time off when I was forced to stop because my body wouldn't work anymore. My career was stressful and I was gaining weight annually. As I started to become aware of this stirring in me, I wondered why I was living such a fast-paced, stressful life and what I was trying to prove.

Seeing my mother and having that thought—*you can't take it with you when you die*—jarred me into realizing what is really important in life. I felt the start of my fast-paced life catching up with me, and I felt overwhelmed with grief. There is no rehearsal for death. No preparation at all. Not like a wedding. Nothing prepares us for how to handle loss or how we will feel when grief strikes, yet it's inevitable that we are all going to experience this in life. We all have a finite amount of time on this earth, yet I had become so disconnected from this reality while living my busy life and avoiding giving myself the treasured gift of living a healthy lifestyle daily.

My mother's death was a big wake-up call for me. In fact, it was the start of a deeper inward conversation about what my life was really all about. Why was I living such a fast-paced life with so much stress? I wasn't happy with carrying excess weight, which was 30 pounds at my heaviest, and not taking care of myself on a regular basis. Still, it remained something I was in and out of. It's something I call yo-yo self-care, along with yo-yo dieting. I was certainly not accustomed to making myself a priority. It seemed normal to take care of anything and everything else, which took away the focus on myself.

Just 21 months later, on a Monday around 8:00 a.m., my brother called me. It was unusual for him to call me at that hour. He told me he had bad news. I thought he was going to tell me he was terminally ill or something like that. That would have been awful news for sure, but he told me my father was dead. He had been speaking with him just three hours earlier from the States. My dad told my brother he wasn't feeling too good and that he couldn't speak for long. We later learned that his neighbour saw an ambulance pull up and take him. She called my niece to notify her. She went to the hospital and was told my dad died of a heart attack.

My relationship with my father was so much closer than with my mother and it hit me hard. The grief was more than I could bear. I just couldn't get my head around it. Not only did my siblings and I have a funeral to arrange, we also had to deal with our family home. Thankfully my parents were not packrats but nonetheless, there was a lot to deal with. Accepting the reality of the situation and dealing with grief is certainly enough to handle. Dealing with getting the house ready for sale and going through each personal item one by one was really hard, especially with not having the luxury of living close by and being able to take our time.

When I returned home to the States, I felt so empty. I loved my dad so much. I wouldn't be able to pick up the phone and speak with him. I wouldn't get another birthday card or Christmas card. We used to call him "the card man" because he thought a card was so important. He would always make sure he sent it in plenty of time. The sadness penetrated so deep and it consumed me. My husband was so supportive. Without him, the experience would have been even more difficult. I seemed to manage to get through the day, but at night when we sat down to dinner I would cry. This went on for about five months. Grief is so exhausting.

I eventually became curious about grief counseling and decided to go for a session. It was alright but I knew the healing came down to me and it was going to take time. I didn't want more sessions and to start using it like a crutch. I wanted to honour the process by taking it one day at a time. I didn't realize it during the darkness, but the death of my parents became a huge spiritual growth spurt for me, and the pressing purpose of not pushing so hard in life started to become more evident. I felt the need to feel, and to treat myself better, giving space to grieve and having what is really important in life start to surface. That dark time opened me to exploring what my own life was about and why I was here on earth.

I continued to observe the shifts that were taking place in my life; my old ways were still present though. My husband and I used to sit down every night with a glass of wine and just talk. Our conversations would be about anything, and often involved intellectual topics. I knew that drinking every night wasn't good for me, but because I wasn't thinking about drinking morning, noon and night, I considered it just a social thing my husband and I shared. I felt it helped calm my nerves, especially after a hard day's work. It wasn't until a personal diagnosis in the summer of 2011 that I realized I needed holistic change. That diagnosis became the catalyst that changed it all for me, and put an end to my lack of ongoing self-respect, self-care and self-love.

In June 2011, I went for my annual GYN appointment. Every year after each appointment, I received a card in the mail saying everything is normal and go again the following year for my checkup. During this visit the doctor asked me if she had ever told me that my uterus seemed enlarged and then suggested I have an ultrasound performed to see what was going on.

After she received the results her assistant called me to say that I needed a follow-up appointment. I was told not to worry. Of course I was worried. What could it be if it wasn't anything to worry about? During this appointment I was told I had two uterine fibroids, one of them the size of an orange. I was horrified. I felt dirty and flawed. It seemed like my doctor was speaking a foreign language to me because I was having trouble taking it in. I remember realizing I was in shock and if I didn't write down what I was being told I would not remember.

She said I had four options. The first word out of her mouth after that was a hysterectomy that could be done laparoscopically if I had it done sooner rather than later. I couldn't believe I was being told about having a hysterectomy. My mother had a hysterectomy when she was 51 due to cancer. My doctor was telling me that I didn't have cancer. This option seemed so huge. I didn't even know I had fibroids. I wasn't in any pain. It all just seemed too much to take in. Before I could really absorb the magnitude of what I was being told, she told me about two other surgical options that I had never heard of. I wrote them down so I could do the research. The fourth option was to do nothing.

While driving home, the reality hit me and I pulled onto the side of the road to cry. It wasn't cancer or life threatening so why was I so upset? I'd never had surgery before and this seemed like a big deal. I remember feeling like I had let myself down. I was still ignoring the needs of my body. I had pushed it to its limits too many times. The signs were there but I wasn't listening. My body would never let me down, or so I thought.

I got home and later that evening I researched the other two surgical options; I was not impressed at all. I felt so afraid of going under the knife. There was a risk that a hysterectomy could still be necessary depending on the unfolding of these procedures. I felt like they were all invasive and I didn't want my body tampered with. Dental work was the extent of my experience and I wanted to keep it that way. Doing nothing wasn't an option for me. I knew that these fibroids didn't belong in my body and I knew that I wasn't going to opt for surgery without exploring other options first. Surgery would be my last resort if absolutely necessary. I have always erred on the side of doing things naturally when necessary and I've never been a big pill popper. Even during my times of recuperating from exhaustion it was a question of rest and not a question of pills.

I immersed myself in finding a holistic approach that would aid in shrinking the fibroids naturally. I discovered that my hormones needed to be balanced and I embarked upon a Hormone Rejuvenation Program that spanned over three cycles. Little did I know at that time what a major shift it would create in my life and that it would serve as a catalyst for permanent healthy lifestyle changes.

One of the big requirements for a successful outcome was a three-month endocrine rebuilding diet. This involved eating as much organic food as possible, and eliminating alcohol, caffeine and unfermented soy as they affect the thyroid gland. I wasn't a big fast food person, but my eating habits certainly needed some help. I also had to decide what to let go of emotionally and physically in my life so I could reduce my stress levels in a healthy way. I jumped in with both feet and gave it my all for the duration of the program. In addition, I had to rub three different homeopathic creams on different parts of my body at different times of the day and put drops under my tongue to balance my hormones. The process was very involved. My love of spreadsheets came in very handy! It was the perfect solution to keeping everything organized.

During this time, I realized how much I was loving giving myself this personal attention of nurturing my body, and honouring it the way it deserves. I remember thinking that my car got better treatment over the years than my body did. It was such a revelation to acknowledge that my body is my ultimate vehicle and indeed a priority. Without it I couldn't go anywhere, just like when I was exhausted and forced to rest. The holistic approach I chose to heal my body wasn't a chore at all even though it was involved. Every time I applied the creams or took the drops, I felt empowered by taking care of my needs. It felt good to take charge of myself. My life slowed down. I was no longer in a rush and going a hundred miles an hour.

Suddenly, without effort, when I made those lifestyle changes and focused on what mattered in life—my health, self-care and holistic well-being—I found myself losing weight without dieting. I started to enjoy cooking more. This put an end to eating out several times per week and drinking wine most nights because my new ways became a habit. Cooking was a way to decompress and escape from the demands of my day. I was receiving numerous compliments from people about how well I was looking and how much slimmer I was. For the first time in my life I was making myself a priority daily and I kissed goodbye to the excuses that had hindered taking care of myself for over two decades. I finally understood putting my own oxygen mask on first. It was an epiphany. After years of yo-yo self-care and yo-yo dieting, here I was looking and feeling so much better than I had in years. I decided that it was time to change my ways and the uterine fibroids provided the perfect opportunity.

The fibroids didn't completely disappear but they did start to shrink. What really got my attention was that by focusing on my health, weight loss happened naturally without deprivation, rules and restrictions. I had not discovered this previously because I was brainwashed by diets, the next one being the knight in shining armour that would come to my rescue.

I wanted to share my new-found success with others. It seemed like such a natural step on my journey because I know all too well that it is an area of struggle for so many people. I went from a stressful, fast-paced life to one of self-care. To share with and support others, I became a board certified holistic health coach and the author of, *Stop Dieting Start Living: 5 Foundations for Your Health to Permanently Lose Weight Without Dieting, Starvation or Suffering in Silence.* Helping people make the lasting, permanent changes I have made in this area truly feeds my soul.

It's in sharing my story, and now supporting those on the journey to permanent change that lifts and lights me. Recently, I was interviewed on the Law of Attraction Radio Network, a radio show reaching over seven million people around the globe, unified in a message of well-being. I shared with the audience the pillars of my work, experiences with yo-yo dieting and the path to permanent self-care. Changing anything in your life is like building a new house; you can't put up the roof until you have the walls, and you can't put up the walls until you have the proper foundation.

For me, it took moments of total grief and despair, and the journey to holistically heal my body, to transform a stress-filled life to one of true self-care. I felt devastated by my parents' deaths and, reminded of life's fragility and what really matters, my own health challenge became the catalyst for my change. Now I'm so blessed and honoured to support others to stop the self-neglect merry-go-round and embrace permanent healthy changes in their lives.

CREATING MY SWEET & DEADLY LIFESTYLE

Calli Jensen

My final nights in Vancouver were spent sleeping on an air mattress in the middle of my empty condo, surrounded only by the terrible memories that I allowed to happen. I had to sell everything to raise enough money to move, walking away from everything I had ever known. I gave up all my personal belongings, spending evenings bawling and telling myself my new truth: I would never let myself get to that point again. This was definitely the burnout in my life.

From a young age, I learned a lesson I would later have to reverse; men left me. In my earliest years, my father Bob left us. My mother Judi worked so hard to give me an amazing life, always working four, sometimes five jobs, to provide for me. Whatever had to be done to give me everything I needed, my mom did it. If Mom wasn't cleaning houses, she would be cutting hair, working in a funeral home or taking care of mentally challenged children. I remember going with her to work in a group home. To this day, I'm forever grateful for that. I learned about being an entrepreneur and being self-sufficient; at the age of 16, I started a business cleaning fish tanks and breeding reptiles, early beginnings of my entrepreneurial life.

After my father left, my grandfather Rodney became the father figure in my life. During summers I stayed with him so my mom could work and go to school. We bonded so much, especially with my horse riding lessons. He used to drive me every weekend, then pick me up afterwards and listen as I told him all the amazing things I learned with the horses that day. One particular day, I was waiting, and waiting—surely he would pick me up soon? I was so excited to tell him about my day. He never came though. My grandpa had suffered a heart attack and died, leaving me with a mental scar for a long time.

It was years later, and carrying the weight of these early ages, I plummeted to the lowest point in my life. Drugs became my habit, an escape I resorted to, what I thought of as a party lifestyle, but really it was the easy way out. I felt like something was holding me down and I tried to escape reality instead of dealing with life.

In 2009, I was in a car accident on the night of Halloween. I rear-ended the truck in front of me after he slammed on his brakes; there was no way for me to stop in time. My good friend, seven or eight months pregnant at the time, was sitting shotgun and just in the nick of time I put my arm out to stop the airbag from hitting her stomach. I remember reaching out to my father for help; he told me he had just spent too much money renovating his kitchen and wouldn't be able to help us. Meanwhile I was putting my mother through hell and I was in no position to pay the $9,000 to fix my vehicle.

It was right around that time, I was really struggling with my father not being around, so I decided to write him a letter. I put everything I had to get out in that letter, and some things I probably should have kept to myself. A few of the main things I said to him were that I didn't ask him to leave and miss all of my growing up; my first steps, all the way to graduation. I was so hurt he was never there for me and my mother and I told him if he wasn't going to be my father, why did he have me? For years I battled this question. Why did my father not want me?

I didn't realize it when I sent that letter, but he was on his deathbed, and his wife at the time read it to him then. Those were the last words spoken to my father. He passed away just shortly after my accident. I never got to say goodbye one last time. I wasn't invited to the funeral. My auntie mailed me an obituary with our family crest and a small pin with the Campbell family colours. I was completely devastated.

As years went on, I was in and out of abusive relationships, which put me under a lot of stress. I also worked in a toxic environment and was belittled by a man in the office. At the same time, my health was really deteriorating. I was constantly sick, missing work a lot. I had fainting spells and problems with my stomach, going to several doctor's appointments, but they couldn't determine what was causing all my issues.

My health just worsened over time. As I was getting ready to go to the closing ceremonies for the 2010 Winter Olympics, I fainted in the shower and woke up covered in blood. I had broken my nose and cracked my tooth in half; my jaw was out of place and I didn't know where I was. The next thing I knew I was in the emergency room. I was having some type of attack and pains in my stomach. After several doctor's appointments and tests like colonoscopies and biopsies, they said I was going to be okay.

All the while, I self-sabotaged relationships that were important to me, thinking they would eventually leave me one day. My drug addictions got really bad, partying every weekend and doing drugs to escape dealing with my reality and responsibilities. I was addicted to crystal meth and then cocaine and the addictions were ruling my life.

Beneath everything, I knew I had to make a major change or I may not wake up one day. I didn't realize the biggest problems were my choices, environment, stress and substance abuse, and not wanting to deal with major health issues. I remember one night in particular; I knew things had to change. I was driving escorts and selling drugs to make ends meet to survive. I sat in my car in North Vancouver with my Jack Russell Terrier, Mylo, waiting for the escort to finish with their customer. Mylo and I waited until noon the next day, me doing drugs and him looking at me with big puppy eyes—when would we be going home? When we did get home, I didn't have food for Mylo and my power was cut off. I was feeding my own addiction rather than paying my mortgage, bills and food. I had no idea I was slowly killing myself.

I soon found out I had abnormal cells in my cervix and six lumps in my breasts. They immediately treated me for both, which I had to deal with every six months. It was a traumatizing time, treatment after treatment exhausted me, and I was concerned about losing my job because of my health issues. I had the lumps removed and got implants to help with insecurities about my body. At that point in my life, I hated myself, destroyed the relationships around me, and hurt the person who I loved for many years.

The last person I foolishly trusted really took advantage of me. Somehow in the mix of all this, I had opened a clothing store. Within the first year, I hired an assistant to help me run it and she knew I had just come into some money. At the time I didn't know they were related, but a man from her family came into my store one day with his father. The man told me he was dying, saying he had almost died in a car accident caused by a drunk driver, and that he had a tumor the size of a football. He said if I helped him out, he would pay me from his large settlement. I later felt he was always watching me, planning this, and even though I helped him, I allowed him to rob me. The whole time in the presence of this family, I was scared for my life. They threatened me several times with the Red Scorpions gang and Hells Angels. He said if I didn't do what he said, he would make sure I disappeared like the others before me.

This man forced me to take all my money out of the bank, which was to help pay for my clothing business and condo. Within the course of a week, I was completely broke and seeking police protection. His whole family were professional fraudsters and well-known to the police. He had broken into my home, stolen my car, sexually abused me and took all my savings to the point where I couldn't keep my condo. While I was at the police station, he had gone into my home and took all my important documents. The sequence of events from there just got worse and worse.

My mother was petrified for me. She drove the 10-plus hours from Alberta to help me change the lock on my condo and recover my vehicle from police. She then took me to the hospital for HIV and rape testing. My mother dropped everything to be there for me. I had lost everything; my condo I had purchased at 24, and my new clothing store that wasn't even open a year. That was the last straw. I had to lose everything to have my wake-up call. I had to change or I may end up on the streets... or worse.

A good friend of mine, Anil, was moving to Toronto for business. He was the only person other than my mother that was there for me and helped me deal with all this. I decided to get away from all of it and drive him to Toronto. He has been a great support in my life and the one person I feel I can trust. Anil and I are now dating and have been doing some amazing things in life and business together; he has been my rock.

After I dropped Anil off in Toronto, I went back to Vancouver to pick up the rest of my stuff. I was changing my life for good. Two days before I moved, I met my brothers Jason and Jonathan, my sister Lisa, my auntie Sharon, and my uncle Allan, my dad's brother, who I had been searching for over 15 years. Meeting them meant so many unanswered questions were answered and I felt a sense of being again. I met my whole family for the first time in years and it completely changed my life. A part of me that was missing for so many years became complete. The one thing I promised myself was that if I was leaving to drive across the country, I was going to find my father's grave to say goodbye and also find my siblings. I felt so blessed and grateful to have finally found them. I would not have ever crossed their path if the timing and all the signs weren't pointing me in their direction.

It was a long drive after just having driven from Vancouver to Toronto three weeks earlier, then turning around to drive back. I must've been nuts, right? I had a plan to have everything complete in one month to sell all my things. I sold some things and gave the rest away, hitting the road right before winter began.

The day I was leaving for Toronto, I went for an MRI and they found more lumps in my breast and a six millimeter lump on my liver. When I found that out, I knew enough was enough. The changes in my life were necessary not only for my life to get back on track, but also to get my health back.

I had finally realized that until I make major changes in my life, nothing else around me would change. The pain I was in was unrelenting, forcing me to change. The day I started to let go of all the negative—those things I had created from my own actions—my whole world shifted for the better. When I left Vancouver, and the devastating lifestyle I had created, every ounce of my life started to change in a positive way. It was incredible. My journey to a new life in Toronto had begun.

It was a long drive, just me and Mylo, knowing I was now making a positive choice to change. It took me one week to make the drive. I stopped and met more family, learning my family history and spending time with my auntie Eileen. We looked at old pictures of my dad and great great grandparents. In this adventure I found a sense of self like a butterfly emerging from its cocoon. I started to know who I was, and who I was meant to be, in order to share my story and empower other women in their lives.

My family lineage is Rob Roy McGregor. He is the Braveheart of Scotland who fought for the people. It has taken me a long time to find my purpose in life, but now I know I must carry out that name and become the strong woman I have felt in my heart my whole life.

The biggest lesson I learned on my journey is not to hold onto certain things that cannot be changed. Reliving the past over and over was not allowing me to receive the breakthroughs I needed to become the woman I am meant to be. I now know that I had to become a brand new person to create new and better outcomes.

It's been a year since those last nights in my condo before I changed everything. Since leaving my old self, desolate and desperate in those lowest moments of my life, and choosing to make real, powerful changes, my life has completely turned around. I have re-launched my clothing line, Sweet & Deadly Online, and I am starting to be an example who empowers women all over the world. I surround myself with amazing women who inspire and challenge me to become who they know I'm capable of becoming. My health has improved and I'm blessed to be writing a chapter in this book. It's really hard sometimes when you are your own biggest enemy. I didn't realize I was slowly killing myself inside and out by not dealing with my challenges. Facing problems and dealing with them head on is the only way to truly transform—and I have learned that when you do that, everything opens up. I've experienced near miracles and opportunities that did not exist before, the universe giving me all the things I have asked for.

Since moving, both my businesses are doing exceptionally well and the growth is so exciting. I am working with amazing mentors like Claudia Harvey, a renowned businesswoman and consultant whose company's product has launched and excelled in major retail chains across North America and Australia, and Greg Turner, a digital marketing mastermind, both of whose expertise is helping to take my business to the next level. Every choice I've made has empowered me to get to this place. I am so blessed and now train people for our company on social media; once the student, now the teacher.

There's a great joy in succeeding—and in seeing customers so happy with the results they get, specifically from my Sweet & Deadly Waist Trainers. A customer and friend Brenda, for example, recently contacted me with so much excitement. She has dropped 30 pounds since she started using the waist trainer and, along with clean eating, has lost 11 inches around her waist overall. It's not the weight, necessarily, it's the knowledge that I am making a difference in women's lives. They are satisfied with their success and health, and this is what gets me out of bed each morning.

I am now also a Luxury Consultant and Brand Partner with Global Wealth Trade, which allows me to provide Luxury Fashion in addition to my Sweet & Deadly fashion business to clients all over the world. Empowering women to succeed in business, and in living a healthy lifestyle with my waist training products, has meant I've been able to impact a lot of women in a positive way. The best part is building relationships with all these wonderful women and seeing their transformations.

While on my journey, I've also learned to start trusting men, allowing them back in my life in a positive, healthy way. I know that to empower women, I must also acknowledge and empower men with me as an example of a powerful woman. When my dad and the man who took advantage of me did what they did, I formed an opinion of men that resonated through my life in my choices and actions. I had to learn that what my dad and that man did had nothing to do with me. They just did what they did, and being a victim around that had left me disempowered in my own life to create what I want.

It was a lack of trust from abandonment, feeling used and unloved. I created those stories and drama and made it my reality without realizing how deeply it would radiate within me. These internal feelings also created my illness, pain and discomforts that could have killed me.

I realize now, more and more every day, that I am not stuck in anything. My past is not my future. By being present to living in the now, and working on myself with what I want, I keep from repeating my past so I don't put it into my present or my future. The worst feeling is when you feel like giving up and you don't know how much longer you can fight for your life. Let me be the proof that you can pick yourself up and keep going! I know now: you can be the person you've always wanted to be!

FROM FEAR TO FREEDOM

Natalie Marnica

A coin toss. That was what my life had come down to. When I was 20 years old I found out my mom was ill. She has a hereditary brain disorder called Huntington Disease that would eventually consume her. I was already familiar with this,having watched my grandfather seemingly disintegrate before my eyes and now I would watch my mom do the same.It was one of the first times I understood there was more to be frightened of besides death. I had a 50 percent chance of inheriting the gene.

As time went by, the roles of my mom and myself started to reverse. She slowly became more dependent on me and increasingly I took on her responsibilities. Within five years I became the "mom" in my family with all the duties of an adult without having the skillset. To make matters worse, during this time I was in a car accident that left me feeling pain constantly. I was unable to work or be active and started to isolate myself from others.

Every day, every moment, I felt overwhelmed, often dealing with my mom with harshness and rage. I remember screaming at her in frustration when she would do something I didn't understand. In the early stages of the disease she often took our dog Ali for walks.

One day I was watching her from our balcony. My mom was blindly following Ali as she sniffed around the grass. While my mom looked dazed and unaware of her surroundings, the dog slowly made her way towards the road. The cars were quickly driving by. My heart was racing and my hands were tightly clasping the cold, metal rail. I could feel overwhelming fear that she would get pulled across the busy road. My body trembled as my mom stepped closer to the curb. I screamed out to her but she couldn't hear me. Luckily the drivers stopped when they saw her and the two of them daintily crossed the street, still unaware of the dangers that could have befallen them. I was relieved, but still felt so angry at what I saw as her carelessness.

When she came back upstairs I met her in the hallway. I screamed furiously at her—"how could you be so careless?" She was totally oblivious to what I was saying. She just looked at me with tears in her eyes and began to apologize. Guilt immediately flooded over me. I ran to my room, slammed the door and fell to my knees weeping. How could I be so cruel to her? This wasn't her fault. I was so scared that she could have been hurt and I was so mad that I couldn't have stopped it. I had no control. That was the real problem I faced; I had no control over this disease, or over her eventual death. I was a wreck. Underneath it all, frightened by the very possibility that I too would manifest this disease.

Fear of illness crept into my relationship with my partner. The person who was my best friend now became the target of all my aggression. The stress I felt with my mom meant I had no patience with him and I was always quick to anger. The fear of illness became a part of my identity. I saw myself more and more as a victim of life, being dealt one shitty hand after the other. *Why is this happening to me?* provoked my repeated thought pattern. I was stuck in a body that felt broken while caring for a sick parent who was progressively getting worse. I felt pain in my whole being. No longer could I feel or express joy. I closed myself off, especially from friends, and kept everything a secret. Fear made my life very small. At the same time, I was desperate for hope, wishing there was something or someone out there who could fix it.

One day while reading a vitality magazine I noticed an ad for a sweat lodge ceremony. It intrigued me. Out of desperation for change I called the number to inquire, took a leap of faith, and decided to attend the next sweat. Two weeks later I arrived at the gathering and sat nervously on the couch as the rest of the attendees gathered around. The dance chief introduced herself and began to pass around a "talking" stick. Each person began to put their name into the space and spoke about why they were there. I could feel my body trembling and a wave of emotions flooding through me. My hands started to get clammy as I held the stick. The sensations moved up to my chest and throat; I tried desperately to push them down so I could speak.

"My name is Natalie," I said, while trying to ignore the room full of eyes on me. "I am here…" Tears started to rush down my face. "I'm here because my mother is sick…" My body was shaking and I could barely finish my sentence. "…And I don't know what else to do." It was the first time I spoke my fears or allowed others to see my pain. This experience started me on my path to healing. I attended monthly gatherings and prayed for my mom, my family and myself. Being in this community gave me some relief from the demands and stress of my life. I slowly began to feel the first stirrings of hope.

Early in 2009, my aunt invited me to try a yoga class in hopes that it would help relieve my aches and pains. It was hard. At first I didn't feel any better but I persevered. After five or six classes, I started to feel less pain and gain more strength and mobility. About a year into practicing I realized that I wanted to help others find relief for their pain, so I decided to participate in my first yoga teacher training. I also undertook a three-year shamanic program to continue healing myself and prepare for whatever battles would lie ahead. In 2010 I started my business, Sacred Mountain Yoga, which provides therapeutic-based yoga practices and wellness services around the city of Toronto and online. After a few years of teaching I enrolled in a two-year yoga therapist training. I wanted to be able to help other people living with illnesses, especially those with chronic pain and Huntington Disease. The famous yogi BKS Iyengar once said, "yoga teaches us to cure what need not be endured and endure what cannot be cured." I knew that either way, this path was for me.

While yoga and shamanism gave me real tools to improve my life and become a better daughter and partner, I unknowingly started to build a network that would one day support me in the time of my greatest need.

My mom's health continued to decline so my brothers and I came together and started to share the caregiving duties. We wanted to keep her at home with us as long as possible. I was constantly worried about her safety while being afraid for my own future. When I wasn't looking after my mom, I was driving around the city teaching yoga classes and trying to build my business. Stressed by my caregiving responsibilities and the physical demands of teaching, the pain in my body became unbearable. I often woke up unable to move my back and neck. Throbbing pain traveled and radiated throughout my tensed body. I felt I was reaching a breaking point.

I was sitting with my mom one afternoon and, as I clasped her cold, dry hand, I was suddenly overwhelmed with the vision of becoming just like her. I just sat there, looking at her through teary eyes. The woman who was once strong, the caretaker of my family, was now reduced to a state of infancy: needing to be fed, washed, dressed and no longer able to stand on her own two feet. Would this be my fate? To spend my youth easing the suffering of the woman who gave birth to me only to end up being consumed by the same disease? Physically, mentally and emotionally exhausted, my relationship with my boyfriend became untenable. I couldn't move forward while being so afraid of what could come. I felt that the chance I had inherited this illness was more likely than not. I decided that my life would not include marriage or children of my own. I left him, trying to spare him from the pain of having to care for me if I fell ill. I also couldn't concentrate on my schoolwork and I almost left the yoga therapist training program. Believing that it would be to my benefit, my teachers encouraged me to stay and offered extra support. It was one of the greatest gifts I had in my life at that time.

The question of whether I had HD hung like a sword over my head that could suddenly drop. Every involuntary movement or twitch that I felt in my body would trigger the thought that HD was starting to manifest. The fear that lurked below the surface became evermore present. Yet, outside of the sweat lodge ceremonies, I never spoke about it. No one in my family did. It is the ever-present elephant in the room. I reached out to my shamanic teacher to discuss what was happening. She encouraged me to face my fears and take control of my life, offering to guide me along the way. I decided I needed to find out if I was HD positive. The constant questioning and anxiety of not knowing became too much to bear. I decided to get tested in November of 2013.

I told my best friend J Bear what I was doing, although she could see it coming. She sometimes knew me better than I knew myself. We had become really good friends and it is with her that I learned to have some fun again. She brought joy back into my life at a time when I needed it most. It was one of the only times I felt like a normal person. J Bear was with me through it all, from the moment I decided to get tested to when I went to meet with the genetic counselors and now, lending her support while I write this chapter.

By January 2014 my results were in. I remember getting the call. I was terrified and I couldn't deal with it yet. I felt I needed to wait, at least until my mom was in full-time care. I didn't think I could process my results, continue to work and look after her.

Managing my day-to-day life was exhausting. I woke up, practiced yoga, got ready, and made sure my mom was cared for with medications, a bathroom visit and breakfast all before I left to teach. My routine was to rush home after class to prepare lunch for the two of us and then leave again to teach evening classes. One day I was very short on time and rushing to prepare everything before I had to go. My mom was sitting at the dining room table eating her food while I cleaned up the kitchen. I was very tired and overwhelmed, my brain felt scattered. I went to take the food processor downstairs to our cantina and I slipped! My heart jolted and in the blink of an eye I skidded down the cold, ceramic steps and smashed my spine. The processor flew out of my hands and crashed against the floor with a bang. My mom, frightened for me, screamed down to me but I couldn't get up or reply in that moment. We both knew she wasn't able to help me even if I needed it. I yelled up the stairs that I was ok, but I wasn't. Nothing in my life was. I started to sob. My back was throbbing, the sadness and frustration was pouring out of me, I just wanted to scream but I couldn't. I didn't want her to know what was happening to me. After a few minutes I rolled myself up off the ground, wiped the tears from my eyes and went back to my duties.

I couldn't handle it anymore. The pain penetrated every layer of my being. I began to welcome death. I would fantasize about dying. Sometimes I'd be driving home and feel like steering my car into a ditch or towards oncoming traffic, something that would obliterate me. I wanted it all to end. I didn't think I was strong enough to face reality anymore.

Despite the struggle I knew that I wanted to help other people who were like me; depressed, confused, hopeless and desperate for relief. I continued to teach and show up, regardless of the pain. I dreamed of being able to create a wellness program for caregivers and youth who were at-risk for HD. That became one of my goals. I needed to know if I was gene-positive so I could make sure to complete the projects before I wouldn't be able to. I also needed to know whether I could have a family with someone. I had already decided I wouldn't get married or have kids if I was positive. There was no way I would bring another life into this world knowing they would have to eventually take care of me or toss the coin themselves.

With the additional stress of now having my results and not knowing, I felt like I was at another breaking point. It was during this time that the most amazing team of women supported me. My best friend in the whole wide world, J Bear, never left my side. She often stayed with me for days, offering me her shoulder to cry on and making me laugh and smile. My yoga teacher gave me therapy, a soft place to land, when I couldn't afford it. My shamanic teachers encouraged and supported me throughout the process and arranged that I could come and live with them after getting my results, and stay until I was well enough to return home. I kept this a secret from my family, not wanting them to worry or question things.

The date was set for November 12, 2015.I booked a one-way ticket to British Columbia for that very day to go stay with my shamanic teachers. The countdown was on. My good friend Michaela also supported me during the weeks leading up to my departure. One day I showed up at her house looking like a zombie. Michaela took one look at me, put me on her massage table for an energy balancing and let me rest. Her warmth and kindness revived me enough to keep moving forward.

I became determined to take back my power and to control whatever I could to create the life I dreamed of. I wanted to inspire others to take control of their lives, despite their circumstances.

The day finally came. Soon, for better or for worse, I would face my fear. My bags were packed and loaded into my car. Michaela met J Bear and I at the hospital. We didn't have to wait long before the counselors ushered us into the room. "Are you ready?" one of the counselors asked me in a soft and somber tone. I took a deep breath and replied, "I guess so." She pulled a white paper out of the envelope and slid it across the table towards me. "The paper shows the number of repeats for the Huntington gene. If the numbers are 36 or more it will show a positive result, however your numbers are between 18-21, well within the healthy range. You tested negative for Huntington Disease." I was shocked when the words came out. I looked down at the paper to read it again. Michaela was in tears, kissing and squeezing me. The counselor continued to speak but I couldn't hear much at that moment, everything felt fuzzy around me like I was going to pass out. Were all of my fears wrong? All the years I spent analyzing every twitch and tremor, associating it with HD only to learn I was normal? It didn't feel real to me. I asked the counselor, "can you please say that again?" She paused and said, "Natalie, you do not have Huntington Disease." "Again," I said, tears pouring out. "You do not have Huntington Disease." I was utterly shocked and relieved. Within the hour I was rushed to the airport ready to board a plane.

When I arrived at the airport my shamanic teachers greeted me with open arms. They picked me up and I was off to my new home. I kept my results close to me, pulling it out any time I had a twitch to remind myself that I was ok.I slowlybegan to recover from the burnout. It is truly amazing what proper rest and relaxation can do! I developed an even deeper self-yoga practice that supports me in all aspects of my life. Although I still had chronic pain, I began to feel better. I spent time relaxing, hiking and traveling with my housemates. I woke up to kisses from two beautiful dogs. I was empowered by the women in my life that never lost faith in me and supported me throughout this process. Their encouragement kept me alive and gave me strength to hold it together. I was given a chance to write a new chapter of my life.

Now I am actively providing support and helping others to cope with the uncertainties of life. As a Yoga Therapist, I have the privilege of teaching people who suffer from various injuries and illnesses how to improve the quality of their lives. I've also expanded Sacred Mountain Yoga's services to not only include teaching group yoga classes, but providing online training, corporate wellness programs, workshops and seminars. In November 2015 I was invited to share my knowledge of yoga and healing for YPAHD, Young People Affected by HD. This was my first time presenting the yogic view of health to my peers. I shared my experiences in front of young people who were dealing with similar life situations, most of whom were still challenged by the inevitable choice of tossing the coin themselves. I could see myself in them. I talked about the importance of physical exercise, breathing and its effects on the mind and nervous system, creating support systems and making healthy life choices. One young lady came up to me after the presentation and thanked me for inspiring her to keep staying active and pursuing healing for herself and her mother, who was recently diagnosed with HD. I've also become a Mentor with YPAHD in their youth mentorship program and started to create a wellness program for the HD community.

The truth is we can never know what lies in our future or how much time we have on this planet, HD positive or not. Life is fragile and ever-changing. One of the biggest lessons I learned throughout my journey, which spanned nearly a decade, is that creating a network of support is essential for not only getting through the hard times, but also to experience the joys of life. There are angels that walk amongst us, people full of love and compassion, who are willing to be of help if you ask. Good friends, teachers and mentors can enrich our lives immensely!

It's my honour to be able to empower others, to help alleviate their suffering and continue to inspire people to participate in their own rescue, one breath at a time. If I can transform every painful situation in my life into something positive, then all my experiences have been worth bearing.

PERSISTENCY IS KEY

Sabbir Chawala

I fell in love with this beautiful country Canada the moment my little feet stepped out of the airplane. It was 1974 and I was only five years old. Holding my mother's hand, I felt a sense of safety that would guide me through my childhood.

There were going to be challenges on this journey, but I was extremely fortunate to have a very loving mother and a father who would work hard to support our family.

My parents didn't know how to read or write in English and both of them had less than a Grade 5 education, so you can imagine how difficult it was to get accustomed to Canadian society, culture and the language. That didn't stop my mom from doing everything to keep our family together or my father from working seven days a week, 12 hours a day.

My mother always taught us to turn our fears and limiting decisions into a powerful life to help others. I cherished every moment I spent with her. Both my parents worked for minimum wage, but they still sponsored two children in India to give them a better life, even though we were struggling here in Canada. My parents taught us that every gift they gave brought at least as much happiness to them. To this day they continue to give and help the poor and needy back home in India.

As a child I was put in special learning classes because of a learning disability and I had challenges communicating with other people. A lot of young kids are afraid of talking, but having to learn a new language made it that much more frightening. I was always afraid to ask questions in class in case it was a stupid question where all the other kids would make fun of me. All of this resulted in me failing Grade 3. Back in the eighties, there was no option to failing, especially in an immigrant family. At first it was a huge deal for my parents; they had to keep it secret from other parents that I failed. They did, however, support me by encouraging me to take summer school and more after school programs. My mom was the one who stood by me during this time, telling me not to worry and to keep moving forward in my education. She has been there for me all my life, supporting what I do and motivating me to keep pursuing my dreams.

My learning disability was a hindrance to me, but my persistence has always been my greatest asset. I learned that from my parents as they always told us that nothing would ever come easy in life and no matter what you're trying to accomplish, it's going to be painful and sacrifices will need to be made. I owe it to my parents to never ever give up.

We moved to Toronto from Montreal in 1989. The benefit of growing up in Montreal was that it gave me the opportunity to learn French. My ability to speak French got me an interview at Dell Computers. I was hired as a bilingual customer service rep and felt truly blessed to have experienced working for a leading multi-million-dollar company.

During the early years in my career, the main secret was to stay humble and not be afraid to ask for help. This helped me get into management positions as I was determined to learn and excel.

Whenever I'm faced with a difficult decision, I ask myself: what would I do if I wasn't afraid of making a mistake, feeling rejected, looking foolish, or being alone? I know for sure that when you remove the fear, the answer you've been searching for comes into focus. My big decision was to go back to India to get married.

I may have been brought up in Canada, but I was still Indian at heart. In 1992, I made my way back to India and got married to my beautiful wife Zarina after spending no more than five minutes together. It was not an arranged marriage, but our families knew each other. Zarina is a very hard-working wife and mother who has done a great job in taking care of our children. She has been my main pillar of success throughout our journey together. We've been married for 23 years and as I write this chapter I reflect on our mutual understanding and respect for each other that has made our marriage so strong for this long.

In late August 1994, God gave my wife and I a beautiful gift, our son Uzair. We were on cloud nine! The feeling of gratefulness and love consumed my soul and I was so thankful to my amazing wife and God that our baby boy was healthy.

From the time Uzair was born, I encouraged my son to do what he loved. All parents want their children to be happy and to be the best they can be. While we can't instill every skill imaginable, there are some essential life skills all parents should teach their kids. I believe that the essential life skills will help our children better cope in the world and grow into responsible, respectful and valuable members of society. My son grew up with great learning skills. Currently as I write this he is in his fourth year at Ryerson University, majoring in Business Administration in project management. Actually I am amazed as he has very good grades, which I didn't have during my school years. My son has won numerous awards in high school, most notably he was awarded the "Crown Attorney Award" by the York Region Justice Department for a Mock Trial Competition in 2012. This is especially dear to my heart because as an immigrant who did not know a lot of English, this beautiful country has given us the privilege to be properly educated. We joke in our family that our son got exchanged at the hospital.

My princess, Azmat, was born on July 13, 2000. Everything was going smoothly in the delivery room, until the very last minute. There were complications that resulted in my wife having to get an emergency caesarean section done. Fear consumed me with the thought that I might lose my wife and my unborn child.

Thanks to the doctors all was well. No Rolex, no Cadillac, no mansion can ever equal the joy of holding your baby girl in your arms for the first time. I cannot describe the feeling that I got on that day when the nurse presented me with my princess. It is a feeling I wish and pray that every man will experience during their lifetime.

At 15 months old, my princess was admitted into the Scarborough General Hospital. She had flu-like symptoms, however the doctors couldn't understand what was wrong with her. The nurses were trying to get blood out of her, but it was not flowing freely from her arms, so they poked her feet and they were able to draw some blood. We waited two hours for the results and the doctor informed us that my daughter's A1C report was 32, her blood glucose reading, which meant that she was diagnosed with juvenile diabetes. If they did not diagnose her when they did she may have died or gone into a coma as the blood was not circulating to her brain. Once she was diagnosed we spent 20 days in the hospital; it was a new lifestyle we needed to adapt to.

When the doctor informed me of the news, my world and my heart shattered. I wanted the earth to stop spinning. My brother in-law Arif Indawala came to the hospital that night and told me to say, "thank you." This took me by surprise so I asked him, "but what am I saying thank you for?" "You're saying thank you," Arif said, "because your faith is so strong that you don't doubt that whatever the illness your daughter encounters, your family will get through it. You're saying thank you because you know that even in the eye of the storm, God has put a rainbow in the clouds. You're saying thank you because you know there's no problem created that can compare to the Creator of all things. Say 'thank you.'"

So I did – and still do. Gratitude can transform any situation. I see hope each time I see my son and daughter.

A diagnosis of type 1 diabetes means your pancreas is no longer capable of producing insulin. We had to do multiple daily injections with insulin syringes, monitoring her blood glucose levels and appropriately administering her insulin. We needed to work closely with our healthcare team to determine which insulin was best for my daughter for the first few months.

Living with type 1 diabetes is tough, but with proper care it can be managed. Balancing nutrition, exercise and proper blood glucose management techniques with the rest of your life's priorities means anything is possible. Our family had to make these adjustments. My son was seven then, but also made sure he adjusted his food intake just for his baby sister.

Every day I was in so much emotional pain. My wife or I had to inject insulin into our little princess; if we didn't she would not live more than three days. During the course of my lifetime I have seen that women, in particular my mother, wife and daughter, have a mental toughness that no man can match. I would make excuses when it came to putting an injection in my daughter as I could not see her in pain. I simply didn't have the courage to put the syringe in her. I have found that women are strong and empowering in that they don't give up easily and will do what's needed to make sure everything and everyone are cared for as they need to be.

In the summer of 2002, we had a near-death situation with my daughter. Low blood sugar, also known as hypoglycemia, can be a dangerous condition. Immediate treatment for low blood sugar levels is important—usually within minutes; if not you may lose the person.

My wife woke up to a loud noise around midnight. She found Azmat screaming as she had a seizure from low blood glucose. My daughter started clawing at me and tried to grab the meter out of my hands. I managed to get her still enough to re-check. It was 2, which is very low and dangerous. I yelled to my wife to bring me the honey as I held my daughter in my lap. I've never seen my son, my wife and I more scared in our lives, but I couldn't let my daughter see that. My wife was crying and begging for God to help. I assured my wife I wouldn't let her go any lower, even though I knew I couldn't guarantee that. Azmat slowly began to calm down and breathe normally, but not to the full capacity. Her heartrate slowed and she became my sweet, loving child again. We quickly called 911, and first responders showed up within minutes. They checked her blood glucose levels in the ambulance, but they could not get a reading. The paramedics administered medicine in the ambulance and again once we arrived in the emergency room. It took hours for my daughter's blood glucose to reach normal levels, and then we were released. These incidents have happened numerous times in her life, however, with each incident she bounces back stronger and healthier than ever.

Today my daughter is 15 years old and in Grade 10. I am so proud of her; even with her medical condition she participates in numerous sports and is doing very well in school. At this young age she continues to live a strong life. Last summer she worked for my real estate business, and as a good father and boss I made sure she got paid. I am so proud of my daughter, but will never forget the day she was diagnosed. I believe that God, no matter what, tries to teach us a lesson every day that brings us closer to him. We've all heard that it's more blessed to give than to receive. Ever since Azmat was 10 years old she has volunteered at the Toronto Sick Kids Hospital and at the Canadian Diabetes Association. I will always look up to her for this, it takes a lot of dedication to volunteer your time, especially at a young age. She is also involved with the Research and Development section at the Sick Kids Hospital. She goes in every three months to give blood so they can see how things have progressed and hopefully one day find a cure.

It is said that anytime we try something that is outside of our comfort zone, we experience growth. During my life the women in my life have helped me change and shaped me to be the better person that I am today. Starting from my mother, my two sisters, my wife and most recently my daughter, they have all shown me courage and have been my pillars of strength. As a Muslim in faith, even the Prophet Mohammed (Peace and Blessing be Upon Him) also found his strength from his first wife Khadija (May God be pleased with her).

Children are a blessing and a privilege; I am thankful to God that I have a million-dollar family. Parenthood should be a source of happiness and wonderful fun. It is also a duty, one of the most serious that you will ever undertake. Do it well and the benefits last a lifetime.

I look at my children for inspiration and motivation. When I was working full-time in IT, I was doing some real estate investment on the side. What I really wanted to do was get my real estate license so I could make my own brokerage and become my own boss. To get your license, all you have to do is take six courses and pass an exam in each course. Seems easy right? To some it is, but for me it was the time where my childhood challenges came back to haunt me. To pass each exam, you had to get 75 percent or higher. In total, I failed 14 exams through the six courses. Many times I got a 74 percent or 73 percent; one question away from passing. Every time I failed, I had to retake the course and then redo the exam. This cost me a lot of money, since you had to pay every time you take a course. I felt like giving up so many times, but the words my mother told me when I was younger rang through my head, "nothing would ever come easy and no matter what you're trying to accomplish, it's going to be painful and sacrifices need to be made." I also continued to try my best to pass because I didn't want my kids to see me give up. I did finally pass all the exams and was awarded my real estate license! So many hours of studying finally paid off and I could start my own business.

Today I am the broker and owner of Century21 Innovative along with my partners. Within six years of our operation we became a Top 10 brokerage within Century21 Canada. We have won numerous awards including the Grand Centurion, the Platinum Award, the Chairman's Club Award and the Top 10 Offices in Canada within Century21. As we continue to grow our business we do not forget to give back to the community. As Winston Churchill said, "we make a living by what we get, but we make a *life* by what we give." With this philosophy we started the Century21 Innovative university scholarship grants for students enrolled in university. My wife and I also started by giving back to our roots back home in India to underprivileged children for higher studies. Society and the world will be a better place when we all get together and educate our children.

My brokerage now has 210 realtors, 20 percent of which are women. I love teaching my values and leadership to all of my realtors; I want to see them succeed while they are a part of my brokerage and encourage them to grow their careers in real estate. I had this one woman who applied to be our receptionist. During the interview I asked, "where do you see yourself in three years?" She responded with, "I want to become a real estate agent." I told her that if she got hired, I would help her achieve her goals. When she got hired, I told her all the steps she needed to take to get her license, and guided her through the process. I provided any resources that she needed to help her succeed. A year later she got her license and is now a successful realtor.

I also had two part-time realtors work for me at the same time. One of them worked full-time with IBM and the other worked in a pharmaceutical company. Both were making very good money in their full-time jobs, but their dreams were to become realtors. I showed them how to prospect, how to cold call and how to get clients. Two years later, they both quit their jobs at IBM and the pharmaceutical company to pursue successful careers as real estate agents.

These are just three of the many examples I have of helping female realtors achieve their dreams. Like I said before, I want to make sure I provide all of my agents with anything they need so they can become successful realtors on their own. To further help the process I have started weekly courses to train realtors and show them the path to a successful and fulfilling career.

Throughout my time, my experiences have shaped me into the person that I am today. I have learned that to achieve I must separate myself from the crowd and be willing to persevere and pursue my dreams with all I have. My parents and the women in my life taught me to strive for more and to work hard, set goals, exceed expectations and work harder than anyone else. The world is full of acres of diamonds, go out and find yours!

THE GIFT OF ADVERSITY

Jennifer Douglas

Irv: Derice, a gold medal is a wonderful thing. But if you're not enough without one, you'll never be enough with one.
Derice Bannock: Hey coach, how will I know if I'm enough?
Irv: When you cross that finish line tomorrow, you'll know.
~ Cool Runnings (1993)

My four-year-old self is running outdoors in freshly cut grass, towards the giant willow tree in the field behind my family home. My favourite thing to do is swing on the lush branches. All the kids in the neighbourhood are out enjoying the carefree innocence of childhood in the early eighties, way before smartphones and social media. Echoes of children giggling and playing flood the neighbourhood. I am blissfully oblivious to the rampant allergens causing my airways to close. Suddenly I am coughing, wheezing and desperately gasping for air. My mom sprints from the backyard and helplessly watches me struggle to breathe. I pass out from lack of oxygen. My mom rushes me to the emergency room.

~~~

After many experiences like this, I was ultimately diagnosed with the most severe type of childhood asthma. For the first 12 years of my life, I averaged about four hospital stays per year. At the age of six, I experienced an asthma attack that nearly took my life; by the time I made it to the emergency room, my nail beds were blue and my lungs were collapsing. It took intensive IV treatment and over a week in the hospital for my condition to improve. When we were out of the woods, the pediatric asthma specialist told my mom, "based on all the asthma attacks I've seen, on a scale of one to 10, that was an eight." My mom asked what a 10 looked like, and the doctor replied, "you don't want to know." After that incident, the doctor said I would never lead a normal life. I was cautioned from participating in a long list of activities that could trigger my asthma.

As a young child though, despite my severe asthma diagnosis, I craved physical activity. One of the activities I loved most was swimming; both of my older sisters spent their childhood as competitive swimmers, and I idolized them for it. I was also inspired to swim during one of my hospital stays, after a terrible attack. I was eight years old, watching the 1988 Summer Olympics from my hospital bed, and I remember my mom telling me, "watch this race. This is Janet Evans from the United States—you won't believe what an incredible swimmer she is." Janet Evans went on to win three gold medals and I thought, I want to be able to swim like that one day.

Not long after my hospital stay, I begged my mom to let me join the local community swim team. Despite fear and hesitation, she called our asthma specialist, who told her swimming is an ideal sport for asthmatics as the-re are little to no allergens in a pool environment and swimming increases lung capacity. "As a parent," he said, "you will need to understand that she will never be able to keep up with the normal kids, but you have no reason to keep her from participating." So with the doctor's blessing and our expectations set low, off to the pool we went.

I started my journey as a competitive swimmer in April of 1989. The doctor's warning that I would never keep up with the normal kids was an understatement. I was painfully slow, and struggled through practices. One month after joining the team, I was back in hospital following another asthma attack, and ended up missing a month of training. When I returned, I started back at square one. This pattern of improvement followed by health deterioration repeated itself for a number of years.

The pattern eventually evolved into something positive though: my asthma attacks were becoming fewer and further between, and I wasn't labouring as much during training sessions.

By the time I was 12, my health started to improve. That year, I accomplished something I never thought possible; I finished in the medals in the breaststroke events at the winter Provincial Championships. I was overjoyed, yet my thoughts turned self-protective: *shouldn't I just be happy to participate? I must have gotten lucky... surely this won't happen again.* I accepted and believed that I would always be the sick girl who could never keep up with the normal kids. When Summer Provincials arrived later that year though, I performed just as well. I slowly began letting go of my fear of disappointment, and started to see myself as an athlete.

I was also so inspired by our team's National level swimmers; at the 1992 Canadian Olympic Trials, I witnessed one of our team members, Stephen Clarke, in the greatest race I had ever seen. It was the 100-metre freestyle final. Stephen dove into the water and turned at the halfway point of the race in first place. The entire crowd rose to their feet with a deafening roar and cheered Stephen to a finish. When he touched the wall in first place, every single member of our team completely lost it. It was such a pinnacle moment—we were a group of kids from the suburbs with hardworking parents who often made great sacrifices for us to be in an organized sport—we had just witnessed one of our peers qualify for the Canadian Olympic Team. Watching Stephen win that race changed me as an athlete. For the first time in my life, I believed in having dreams and goals.

The following season, many more inspired my journey. My father, who had always been an inspiring supporter, really started to vocalize his belief in my potential as a swimmer. His words still echo in my head, "you know dear, I know you don't realize it, but your asthma has made you really tough. You can compete at the National level if you put your mind to it."

He never pressured me, but his constant messages of positive reinforcement were hard to ignore. If anyone knew what it was like to be resilient in the face of adversity, it was my father. He was diagnosed with a rare, inoperable, terminal cancer in 1988. In his doctor's words, "cancer would kill him eventually, but if he remained positive, he would have many years left to enjoy his life." My dad's difficult circumstances made his encouraging words very powerful.

That year I spent a lot of time with another athlete, Kristin Keery, who to this day remains my best friend. Not only was Kristin a talented swimmer, she also had a phenomenal work ethic. She regularly said things like, "you have to be dedicated if you want to be successful!" I was also fortunate to work with a new coach to our team, Andy Moss, who didn't view me as a sickly kid with limitations—he believed in me as an athlete. When you're surrounded by such positive, supportive people, it's difficult not to let their attitudes rub off on you. I started to think differently about my sport. What if I stopped thinking of asthma as a limitation and started seeing it as a strength? If I could withstand the physical battle of a life-threatening asthma attack, surely I could conquer any challenge in the swimming pool. So I made a conscious decision. I would let go of my fears and dedicate 100 percent of myself to the sport for an entire year. My decision paid off; that year I qualified for the Canadian National Championships. This achievement marked the beginning of an incredible mental transformation that would define my career as an athlete.

The potential of the human mind is truly intoxicating. Once I figured out how powerful my mind was as a tool, I used it. Every time I was exposed to a new level of competition, it triggered a new goal.

When your dominant thoughts are focused on achieving a goal, your conscious and subconscious actions automatically gravitate towards a successful outcome. The limitations of being asthmatic were no longer part of my thought process. By this point, I only saw myself as an elite athlete.

By the age of 15, I qualified for the Canadian National Swim Team, and competed in my first international competition. My ever-supportive father drove all the way to Atlanta to support me, and I will never forget his words: "when I saw you marching out onto the pool deck in your Canada outfit, it was my proudest moment as a father." At the age of 16, I participated in the 1996 Canadian Olympic Swimming Trials, and gained invaluable experience as an athlete.

When it came time to think about post-secondary education, I started to consider schools in the United States, where athletic scholarships were available. Thanks to my teammate Cindy Bertelink, a talented distance swimmer on a swimming scholarship to UCLA, the coaches there reached out to me. When I visited UCLA on a recruiting trip, I saw an invested group of student-athletes with remarkable camaraderie and a head coach, Cyndi Gallagher, who was a strong woman and not just a coach, but a teacher too. I vividly recall watching the UCLA swimmers compete against another university, where it poured rain for the entire three hours of the outdoor event. Every single UCLA swimmer was out in the rain, happy, and loudly cheering for one another. The athletes from the competing school were miserable and cowering in the locker rooms. After witnessing this event, I knew in my heart where I wanted to be.

After my recruiting visit, Cyndi sent me an email offering a swimming scholarship. Ten years prior, I never would have imagined such an opportunity as a severe asthmatic, but life takes incredible turns if you allow it to. I accepted the offer, and to this day, attending UCLA has been one of the best decisions of my life.

Within my first month of university, I received heartbreaking news. My father's cancer had spread to his kidneys and his health was rapidly deteriorating. My family purposely waited until I completed my final exams before breaking the news to me that my dad was completely bedridden. It was the worst news I had to process in my life. I packed up one year of belongings in only two hours, and took the next flight home.

~ ~ ~

My 19-year-old self slowly inches into my dad's bedroom. I get a glimpse of his frailty and emaciation. At six foot three, my dad weighs roughly 120 pounds. His physical body is weak, but his character is resilient. I spend the entire summer with him, helplessly watching him weaken. Three months later, fall arrives, and it's time to return to Los Angeles. I don't want to leave him. School will always be there, my father won't. From his deathbed though my dad musters up the strength to yell at me, "no! You're *going back!*" There was absolutely no way he wanted me to remain in Toronto when I had fought for my own health for so many years. My dad insists that I board the flight to Los Angeles that fall, and he dies two weeks later.

~ ~ ~

With unconditional support from my family, friends, and UCLA teammates and coaches, I made it through that year doing the only thing I knew how to do: I immersed myself in the escape of the swimming pool, and focused on the 2000 Canadian Olympic Swimming Trials. I didn't know if I had a chance to make the Olympic team, but I knew I had to try.

Twelve weeks before Olympic Trials, I experienced another heart-wrenching setback. During warm-ups at a championship competition, I fully dislocated my shoulder. The orthopaedic specialist determined my cartilage was torn; I could have surgery, which would take me out of the water for a minimum of 12 weeks, or hope, without any guarantees, that my shoulder would heal itself enough to compete at the Olympic Trials. I was devastated. I didn't know how to process losing the two most important things in my world: my father, and my sport. So, surgery was definitely not an option, I was hell-bent on competing.

After 12 frustrating weeks of rehab, shedding many tears, and training without the use of my arms, I was on my way to Olympic Trials. When all was said and done, I placed fourth and sixth in the breaststroke events. Although I did not qualify for the Olympic Team, the amount of gratification I felt for even competing was indescribable. I felt like I had climbed Mount Everest to even compete, and it was the first moment in my swimming career where I realized that true satisfaction comes not from the final result, but from the journey.

I completed my collegiate swimming career at UCLA as a two-year Team Captain and an NCAA All-American. Upon completing my NCAA eligibility, and after re-injuring my shoulder in an ocean swimming accident, I ended up having shoulder surgery in 2002. It was then I decided that I wanted to compete in one last Olympic Trials.

I returned to Canada in 2003 to train with coach Bill O'Toole, who had a phenomenal gift of being able to identify and harness the unique strengths of each of his athletes. Thanks to Bill's leadership, I was able to execute some personal best times at the age of 24. At the 2004 Trials, I qualified as a semi-finalist in my events, but my performance was below par. I had acquired a food-borne illness right before the Trials where my fever spiked to 107, and I lost 15 pounds within a week. I just couldn't regain the strength I needed to compete at full capacity.

I made peace with the outcome of my final competition, and accepted that things happened for a reason. I left the sport with pride. I met my husband that year, and there were new adventures in life to look forward to. It wasn't about how things worked out at my final Olympic Trials; I saw the last 15 years as a package deal. Swimming gave me my health. I made it so much further than I everthought possible from that day in the hospital bed when I was only eight years old.

~ ~ ~

It's late 2013. My new adventures have begun. I give birth to my first child, a beautiful daughter, and I am on cloud nine in love with her. Fast forward to late 2015. I give birth to my second child, a son, and I couldn't be more grateful for and in love with my family.

Two months later, as fate would have it, and as I am writing this chapter, I have to rush my two-month-old son to the emergency room because he is on his fifth day of a high fever. The doctors think it might be viral pneumonia. Fortunately, my son makes a full recovery within days, but it wasn't until I was racing to the hospital at double the speed limit with tears streaming down my face that I truly understand what it is like as a mother to so desperately fear for your child the way my mom did with me for years.

While waiting in the ER with my son, a young mother with a daughter no more than five bypass everyone in the waiting room; her daughter was having a critical asthma attack and on the verge of passing out. My mom had joined my son and I in the ER; she reminds me that my attacks were always that bad. When that young girl finally got some relief from an oxygen mask and medication, I carried my son out of his room, and walk up to her and her mother.

"Hi sweetheart," I say. "When I was a little girl I used to have to come to the hospital all the time for a mask like that. You are being very brave."

The young mother looks at my mom and I with concern in her eyes, and asks, "did you get better?"

My mom responds before I can say a word. "She went on to earn a swimming scholarship to university."

~~~

I am recalling the valuable lesson from my 13-year-old self—when I decided to invest 100 percent of myself into competitive swimming, and see just how far I've come. I dug deep into the lessons of my past, and made a conscious effort to only focus on the positive things in my life. Today, I am a 36-year-old mother of two and, with this chapter, I am achieving my dream of becoming a published author. I am truly grateful for my husband, my mother and father, and my two sisters, Elaine and Lisa, who have been a great support along my journey. I have also worked hard to become a licensed realtor during my mat leave, which has been a very exciting and rewarding process.

A lot of people have warned me that the real estate profession is competitive, and it's hard to build your client base, and that most people who obtain their license end up quitting. They've asked me if I'm afraid the same thing will happen to me. They don't know that they're speaking with a person who was once told by an accredited doctor that I would not lead a normal life, and how I proved him wrong on every level. The gift of my health adversity as a child has given me the perspective as an adult to not fear anything new. If I had listened to everyone over the years who warned me that I might fail, I would never be where I am today. I know without a doubt that I have all the tools to be a successful realtor; because I am passionate about it, and as long as I have my mind as a tool, I know I cannot fail.

The list of things I learned from my journey is extensive. I learned adversity is a gift that we need to graciously accept. Not having my health in the early years of my life allowed me to be truly grateful for every opportunity that swimming gave me. I learned that there is nothing more valuable in life than your health. If a problem can be solved with money, it's not really a problem. I learned that you need to surround yourself with the right people in life if you want to do great things. The people that you invest the most time with in this life will play a significant role in shaping your thoughts. I learned that everyone needs a support system—and you must allow yourself to receive support from those that care about you. I learned that you need to be truly passionate about anything you devote yourself to. I have always loved the water, and I don't believe I would have excelled in a sport that I didn't love. Finally, the most important lesson that I learned from my journey is that the mind is an incredibly powerful weapon. Every milestone in my life was achieved by focusing my mind on a specific goal; nothing happened by accident. The more goals I achieved, the more confidence I built, and the fewer limiting beliefs I had so I could have success in every way along my journey.

LUV SONG –
THE JOURNEY HOME

Marla David

"At the edge of the cornfield a bird will sing with them in the oneness of their happiness.
And the bird song, and the people's song and the song of life will become one."

Song of the Long Hair Kachinas, Hopi

Have you ever heard a song and were transported back to that time? When I hear the Doobie Brothers' 'Listen to the Music,' I'm cruising in my mother's Cougar. David Bowie's 'Ziggy Stardust' takes me back to that third row seat, mid-June, 1974. Robin Sharma writes in his book, *Who Will Cry When You Die*, "music can lift your mood, put the smile back on your face and add immeasurably to your quality of life." David Bowie's passing is a reminder of how fleeting life is, and the importance not to let your music die in you.

I was a lonely, teenage broncin' buck with a pink carnation
and a pickup truck, but I knew I was out of luck the day the
music died

American Pie, Don McLean, 1971

Everyone has a story. My story is my life from my perspective, along my journey. A friend of mine once said, "we all have a song inside of us we should sing every day." Music is soul speech, the universal language. In the film *The Shift*, Dr. Wayne Dyer says, "everyone already knows we came here with music to play." The many songs along my journey, which align most with my soul, my personal playlist, create my *luv song*.

~~~

Gripping the brass rail, I looked out to the landscape and tracks that fell away as the Hiram Bingham train progressed toward Machu Picchu and our anticipated adventure. We passed people working in the fields. Homes were scattered, some so close I could see in through the window openings. Looking down to the left of the tracks, I saw a small white dog sleeping under a bush. Beside it stood a young girl dressed in customary Peruvian clothing from the 1500s, the time of the Inca. She was holding a baby lamb, similar to the girls I saw outside the cathedral in the old part of Cusco. My attention was drawn to the cabin as music filled my ears. The musicians played Santana's 'Oye Como Va.' I turned around with that sweet smile, knowing that I had arrived fully in the present. A mother and daughter, a young couple, and a group of young men swayed, each one in the moment, as I was. I experienced an epiphany, similar to that orgasmic feeling, just after you have gone over the edge and are relishing in the after-bliss. I felt one with God. I saw myself as God sees me and what it must have felt like at birth, when in my purest state—when I was *home*. The rocking motion felt like I was on a magic carpet ride, a beautiful tapestry of life itself. Filled with infinite joy, I realized at that moment what life was about. I had co-created joy and contentment, manifesting a well-lived life, which was none other than my natural state and an expression of who I am and what I desire. In this empowering moment, and feeling such luv and gratitude, I closed my eyes and put my hand on my heart, as everything is magical when you see things with your heart.

You have to believe we are magic
Nothin' can stand in our way
                    Magic, Olivia Newton-John, Xanadu, 1980

It's faith that allows us to live from our hearts, and with confidence to live our deepest passions; travel is one of mine. I embrace new adventures and experiences through the eyes of my inner child, with wonder and curiosity, finding joy in each journey. Making each day matter, I pay attention to what inspires and motivates me, and what's important. Every experience and encounter is an opportunity, as what you put into life you get out tenfold.

I focus on what makes me happy, taking the time each day to nurture myself and tune into my creative side. I live life from the end, or as I like to say, from my eulogy, co-creating my life of passion and purpose. I am determined to leave the world a better place and make a difference by being here, and by being *me*. I am confident and most importantly, I luv myself. I don't have to 'be' anything, or live up to society's version of what I should or should not be or do. I don't live for the expectations of others. Some people may think I'm a 'piece of work,' but I know I'm nothing less than a masterpiece.

Blessed with abundance in my life, I wake each day with purpose, and go to sleep each night with gratitude. The obstacles, adversity, and challenges of my life were part of my growth, along with that one ingredient, self-luv, helping for me to become the empowered woman I am.

You've got to get up every morning
With a smile on your face
And show the world all the love in your heart
Then people gonna treat you better
You're gonna find, yes you will
That you're beautiful as you feel
                    Beautiful, Carole King, Tapestry, 1971

It hasn't always been this way though. There have been dark moments in my life. One February evening almost half a decade ago, as I sat in the corner of my living room, looking at the beauty and elegance, evil was lurking. There was a lump in my throat. My heart was heavy. Tears welled up in my eyes, and then flowed down my cheeks, along my neck and onto my shirt. I could taste them on my lips; salty tears from my soul. As my chest heaved, something caught my eye. Looking toward the doorway, I saw Sunshine, my little RCA Victor dog, walk in ever so gingerly, her tail wagging. I smiled, and scooped her up into my arms, letting her lick the tears from my face and neck. The only red in the room that night would belong to the roses in the vase on the piano, the roses in the acrylic painting on the wall beside me, and the roses in the print on the fabric and carpet of the room. I laid the razor down, and then called 911.

Surreal. This is exactly how I saw things that evening. It was like watching it play out on a screen before me. This was my "Cri de Coeur," or cry from my heart.

> *I look at you all see the love there that's sleeping*
> *While my guitar gently weeps*
> *While My Guitar Gently Weeps,*
> *Beatles White Album, 1968*

There's usually a defining moment or moments in your life, and one of mine came that February night. While music played, the devil was working inside of me, swelling my brain with that self-sabotaging little voice that held me prisoner inside my own head. There is a native Cherokee legend about a fight going on inside of you that goes something like this—you have two wolves inside of you, a good wolf and an evil wolf, and the one that wins is the one you feed. I was feeding the wrong wolf.

It was all there—limiting beliefs, inadequate feelings, low self-esteem, low confidence, despair, hopelessness, shame, humiliation, guilt, failure, grief, and a warped identity. Through the years at various times I suffered from depression, anxiety, nightmares, fibromyalgia, PTSD, but on this night, contemplative suicide. Unbeknownst to my husband, who lay in bed upstairs, a scene was playing out in the living room below. He was jolted out of bed when the lights of the police cruiser pulled into our driveway and the officers came through the front door that I had unlocked for them.

The pivotal moment came when I was sitting with my husband in a room at the hospital. What an awful feeling. Looking at the blank walls, my mind worked overtime. What was I doing with my life? How did I end up here? Why did I feel this way when I had so much to live for? Then, in the quiet of that room something shifted; an emotional shift similar to a huge 'a-ha' moment or awakening. Suddenly I knew I needed to heal. I knew there were lessons to be learned, a purpose in my journey and I had to find out what that was. I had to stoke the embers of my fire before they went out. There were people wholuved me and I owed it to them. Mostly, I needed to become a shining example to my daughters. By focusing on my unconditional luv for them, along with the luv and support of my husband, I found purpose.

> *Oh, mirror in the sky what is love?*
> *Can the child within my heart rise above?*
> *Can I sail through the changing ocean tides?*
> *Can I handle the seasons of my life?*
> *Landslide, Fleetwood Mac, 1975*

What led me to that February evening? I developed a game plan, my own empowerment project, so to speak. I had to face the devil. I had a problem, but I needed to find a solution. I began to untangle those fragmented and dark parts of myself. These frayed threads needed to be either cut off and discarded or sewn back together in order for my soul to become whole. Through discovery I would identify and define the themes of my life, both negative and positive. I would educate myself and learn tools to help me along this new path. I set immediate and long-term goals. Connecting the dots of my past, I began unravelling the tangles, like picking petals off a rose, one at a time, and that ultimately led to my empowerment.

I began with my identity, going back to the beginning of this journey, back before Marla. I was born weighing six pounds, two ounces, and was delivered by my Uncle Willy. He was the only one who knew me as Marla Lori, the names given to me by my adoptive parents, and as Rose, the name given to me by my birth mother.

> *What's in a name? that which we call a rose*
> *By any other name would smell as sweet*
> *Romeo and Juliet, Shakespeare, 1600*

It was never a secret I was adopted, as was my older sister. People most likely figured this out because I have brown hair and green eyes, where my sister has blonde hair and blue eyes. Being adopted raised a hotbed of issues. People can be so cruel, with comments about my parents not being my 'real' parents. This began my warped sense of identity. Why did my birth mother not want me? Did she ever love me while she carried me? How different a life would I have had if I were raised as Rose? I had thought about my soul as Rose, and my soul as Marla, as though they were separate. I've learned my soul is like a pot of soup; each ladle separate, but still part of that soup, so Rose and Marla are one and the same. My birth mother made a choice in her life, just as I've made choices. It took courage for her to do what she did at a time when abortion was frowned on. It's not for me to judge her, and for whatever part she has played in my life, she gave me the gift of life. For that I am grateful.

I focused on other mother influences. Bubie, my mom's mother, was a typical European grandmother with white hair and a large bosom. I still have the little pillow she gave me before she died. Dad's mother, Rose, was a strong woman and the true matriarch of the family. My mother-in-law continually shows me what great character is. My mother's sister, Auntie Lilly spent weekends with us, but lived behind my Uncle Willy's office. A month before Auntie died, she talked of family members coming through her walls. She sent them away, but on that last night she must have gone with them. Auntie was another mother to me, and also my best friend.

My mom, Rose, was the quintessential stay-at-home mom. She would cook in her dress and apron, hair coiffed from the salon. In all her simplicity, she has taught me much. Mom will be 95 years young by the time this is published. She still has a little of her wit and sense of humour, but with the dementia, it's like pieces of her personality are being chipped away a little at a time. She still knows who I am.

> *I've got money in my pocket*
> *I like the color of my hair*
> *I've got a friend who loves me*
> *Got a house, I've got a car*
> *I've got a good mother*
> *And her voice is what keeps me here*
> *Good Mother, Jann Arden, 1994*

Who am I? Obviously my warped sense of self became my reality. I allowed this story to grow and have power over me. I started off just as any other little girl, but at what point did this begin to change? What was my sense of self, my identity? Who did I see reflected in the mirror? What beliefs created the crux of the story I've lived with inside my head? I was shy, not academically inclined, and school was a challenge. Puberty set off new bells—breasts, no big breasts for a little gal of only five feet. I wore braces for almost four years. I was not pretty and smart like my sister, who was a model and an honour student. All this and the hyperhidrosis (brutal sweating) exacerbated my poor body image, attacking my self-esteem. We all know that sexualization of girls, pop culture, and peer pressure affect the self-esteem of most teens, boys as well as girls. They say almost all teen girls want to change at least one aspect of their physical appearance. Look at all those with anorexia or bulimia, like Karen Carpenter, who died at 32 years old. Like other girls, I grew up in the age of the Barbie doll, the perfectly molded societal version of what a woman is supposed to be.

> *I'm a Barbie girl, in a Barbie world*
> *Life in plastic, it's fantastic.*
> *You can brush my hair, undress me everywhere.*
> *Barbie World, Aqua, 1997*

Many girls experience sexual assault of some form. I had an experience in Grade Five. As innocent as the boys were then, they took me down to the furnace room and saw my privates. I felt such shame and humiliation when my dad confronted me when hearing of the incident. I lived with that my entire life. Like other girls, through negative experiences, I felt like a teacup with a crack; you can repair it, but it is never the same. I felt tarnished, broken and unworthy of luv. In hindsight, the memory of the actual incident was skewed by years of internalization, self-blame, and unreliable memory heightened by thoughts of how others thought and felt of me as a result of the incident, all which damaged my psyche and my precious self-esteem. That story did not serve me well. This was a big discovery. I knew I had to learn a new story, and this would be integral to my healing.

Michael A. Singer in his book, *The Untethered Soul,* writes, "there is nothing more important to true growth than realizing that you are not the voice of the mind—you are the one who hears it." I quiet my mind by practicing mindfulness and meditation. I use visualization, relaxation, hypnosis, and past-life regression tapes. The sounds and vibrations of my luv song help me connect to and with my heart and soul, and to source, to heal me. I quieted that self-sabotaging 'little voice' in my head, and learned how I could reprogram the inner self-talk for positive influence of my thought process. I chose to let go of anger, resentment, negativity and anything that doesn't serve me well.

Choice is the biggest freedom we have and is empowering in and of itself. I set goals and choose those things that are most in alignment with who I am and the values I resonate with, to bring about positive change. Forgiveness has also been freeing. I forgive others, as well as myself, as we are human and life is a process. I am no longer shackled to the past, and am kinder to myself.

This new perspective and the tools I now possess, have given me a resilience to deal with the lower vibrational moments in my life. I had pushed the refresh button and began to reset my life. I was taking myself back to who I was—the essence of my soul. I was going *home.* Like Dorothy in the movie The Wizard of Oz, my ruby shoes were with me all along!

As it had shined across him all his life, so understanding lighted that moment for
Jonathan Seagull. They were right. He could fly higher, and it was time to go home.
Jonathan Livingston Seagull, by Richard Bach

I was always a homebody, so my career path was simple. I never wanted to be anything other than a mother. I began working part-time, however, when I was sixteen at the Yorkdale Shoppers Drug Mart store, stocking shelves and on cash. When I quit Seneca College I became a secretary in the buying offices at F.W. Woolworth, and then in the engineering department of Pittsburgh Paints. Moving to Hamilton, Ontario, Canada, after I married afforded me the time to complete and get my Grade Twelve diploma. Then I completed the Real Estate course. Back in Toronto just two years later, I took accounting courses, and pursued my true passion—becoming a mother.

Becoming a mother was denied to me for almost eight years. I felt deficient and thought I was being punished. Tests, biopsies, x-rays, procedures, pills, and appointments, created an emotional roller coaster. At times I felt like a slab of meat. Two adoptions fell through, both after the babies were born, which was hard to bear. More heartache ensued when I suffered a miscarriage. Then, with renewed faith, I finally held a daughter, through adoption. I still have the memory of seeing her for the first time in the nursery at the hospital. The sun was shining through the window and her hair lit up strawberry-blonde. She was a wee thing! I am grateful to her birth mother for giving her life, and giving me the gift of becoming a mother. To my surprise, a month after adopting, I found out I was pregnant. This explained the evening Oreo snacking! After seven months, a long labor and ultimately a caesarian section, I gave birth to a daughter. She was born at the dawn of summer and I spent some peaceful and endearing moments bonding with her as she lay over my heart outside by the pool. Two years passed and I was again blessed, as my third daughter was born, also by a caesarian section. She was a surprise, and a gift to her sisters. We all pampered our little baby.

Although you see the world different than me
Sometimes I can touch upon the wonders that you see
All the new colors and pictures you've designed
Oh, yes sweet darling, so glad you are a child of mine
                    Child of Mine, Carole King, 1970

Thrust into momhood, I was in my element. Homework, after-school programming, appointments and carpooling became the norm. Over these years, I held various portfolios in two women's volunteer organizations, and was on club level to editor of their newsletters on council. I volunteered at the school, running the parent group, specialty lunches and other programs, and took courses in Photoshop and Illustrator to enhance these opportunities given to me. With my natural organizational ability, and new skills from the diverse nature of projects and challenges, I accomplished much. I never considered myself successful though, at anything other than being a mother, and being a stay-at-home mom carried scrutiny according to societal attitudes. This only fueled my already burning fire of low self-esteem. People said I didn't work. Truthfully, I worked very hard, sometimes even going over the top by my standards. Looking back, I see it was important for me to be that perfect mother. My career was raising my daughters; the most gratifying and validating job of my life.

My girls were raised knowing the importance of being luved and the importance of family. We created wonderful memories. My girls jumped in puddles. Clothing can be washed, but the joy of aligning with your inner child is priceless. The girls began to enjoy music, as I do. Oh, the Spice Girls and Backstreet Boys. We also enjoyed quiet times at home, relishing in the unconditional luv and loyalty of our dogs, which brought laughter and lightness into our home. Laughter was always present. No home had more whoopee cushions than we did! The girls went to summer camp too. I never wanted to have regrets for not doing anything for or with them. At the play Mama Mia with the girls and Mom, we celebrated three generations.

And the seasons they go round and round
And the painted ponies go up and down
We're captive on the carousel of time
We can't return we can only look behind
From where we came
And go round and round and round
In the circle game

The Circle Game, Joni Mitchell, 1968

I married at 22 years old with all the hopes and dreams of a young bride. There were many wonderful years, but things change; circumstances change and people change. After almost 25 years, I became a divorce statistic. This choice shifted much. I don't regret the choice, but am sorry for any hurts I may have caused by making it. We all have choices in life, and this was one I absolutely needed to make. It took a lot of thought, time, and courage I didn't know existed inside of me. I knew that part of my story was finished, and I had to move on to follow my destiny.

It's sad, so sad
Why can't we talk it over?
Oh, it seems to me
That sorry seems to be the hardest word

Sorry Seems to be the Hardest Word,
Elton John, 1976

The cord was quickly severed. I lost one whole side of my family, and some friends. I had to mourn what was. Things became difficult and complicated. My sense of family was further fragmented with feelings of abandonment as two of my daughters moved out. Being a stay-at-home mom, I never figured on that. The icing on the cake was being told I had no say in my daughter's life as I was not the custodial parent. The cloak of protection I had been holding for my children was frayed.

No, not I, I will survive
And as long as I know how to love
I know I'll stay alive
I've got all my life to live
And all my love to give and I'll survive
I, I, I will survive

I Will Survive, Gloria Gaynor, 1978

By focusing on the luv in my heart, I learned to heal the hurts from that tumultuous period. It hasn't changed some things, but I feel there is a general understanding. I focus on the positive and revel in the moments I share with my daughters, creating new memories and lasting bonds; sowing seeds that one day I look forward to reaping, as we used to. I have faith knowing time helps, but luv ultimately heals.

As we all moved forward, I remarried. I was fortunate to gain two wonderful stepdaughters. With my husband and partner, we are forging full steam ahead into retirement. On my first birthday we shared together, my husband asked what I wanted. He took me to an open field so I could run free.

You'll remember me when the west wind moves
Upon the fields of barley
You'll forget the sun in his jealous sky
As we walk in fields of gold

Fields of Gold, Sting, 1993

My home is my refuge. I created an environment where I thrive and enjoy all my pleasures and passions. In the summer, I feel the earth in my bare hands while working in my garden. The backyard is my private oasis and country club. I enjoy watching birds and small animals frequent the wild bird feeders outside.

Eight years of summer camp with the lure of the lake, the woods, canoe trips to Algonquin Park where I paddled where Tom Thomson painted his famous "Jack Pine," all contributed to my luv of nature. I am a member of the McMichael Canadian Art Collection in Kleinberg, with works from the Group of Seven. Within clear view of the Tom Thomson shack, I sit beside my tree with the inscription, *For the Luv of Nature,* and my name.

Connecting to nature awakened my senses and helped me heal. I am fascinated by Bernie Krause's book, *The Great Animal Orchestra: Finding the Origins of Music in the World's Wild Places.* He explains how nature has its own music; a pure music as in the chorus of the cracking of a glacier, bubbling streams, the wind blowing and birds singing. Nature has always awed me, not only because of its beauty, but also because it is ephemeral, ever-evolving. Life is also ephemeral, never staying the same, always changing. Bob Proctor says, "change is inevitable, but growth is a choice."

As things change, along with the traditions of Judaism, I am developing my spirituality. I am allowing it to grow and evolve. The origin of my spirituality came from Friday nights at camp. The director would walk the entire camp, all dressed in white, to the chapel. We sat in rows, benches made of huge logs from the trees. As we sang, sitting together among the tall pines, the sun set in the background over the lake. It invoked a feeling of peace.

> *How the winds are laughing*
> *They laugh with all their might*
> *Laugh and laugh the whole day through*
> *And half the summer's night*
> *Dona, Dona, Dona, Dona,*
> *Dona, Dona, Dona, Don*
> *'Dos Kelbl' — (The Calf), Yiddish theater song, 1941*

In a dream I was floating. Arms of light went around hugging me, but kept circling. Like a cocoon they kept on going, glowing, as I was at peace and in a space of luv. I believe I was being cradled or embraced. I felt at one with God, the source of all luv. I felt beautiful, unconditional luv and could have stayed in that state forever, but I awakened. I sat on the side of the bed for a while trying to make sense of what I had just dreamed, what I experienced.

You're in the arms of the angel
May you find some comfort here
Angel, Sarah McLachlan, Surfacing, 1997

I believe life is like a tapestry. We follow our journey, experience the knots and gnarls of life, but on the other side, like a tapestry, it is a beautiful piece of art. My journey thus far has played out exactly as it was supposed to, and I believe the same going forward. I surrender the outcome of my journey to whatever it will bring. I have faith that whatever happens, whether good or bad, it is the process. This sense of detachment is freeing. I have reached a place in my life where I am being guided by something larger than myself.

How everything still turns to gold
And if you listen very hard
The tune will come to you at last
When all are one and one is all
To be a rock and not to roll
And she's buying a stairway to Heaven
Stairway to Heaven, Led Zeppelin, 1971

Muhammad Ali said, "service to others is the rent you pay for your room here on earth." I have been given a life of privilege. I do my best to give back to society, doing some good deed or act of kindness each day, believing the ripple effect of paying it forward will leave the world a better place. Giving is in the very fabric I am made of. I believe part of my purpose here on earth is to help or serve others. Thanks to the people at TD, I have peace of mind knowing I am financially secure and have everything in order. With all my needs met, it was then important to build a lasting legacy, invest in the future and make a difference. Through TD Bank's Private Giving Foundation, my Roses and Rainbows Foundation gives me this opportunity.

I want to live
I want to give
I've been a miner for a heart of gold.
Heart of Gold, Neil Young, 1972

Giving was also important to my father. Dad was overseas in England as a radar mechanic for the R.C.A.F. After the war he became a pharmacist, and went into business with others to form a chain of stores. One day, Dad and his partners merged with another chain, forming the beginning of what we now know as Shoppers Drug Mart, Canada's leading drug store retailer. By the time this will be published, Dad will have been gone over 9 years. His passing thrust me into a whole new world I was ill-prepared for, yet I stepped up to the plate. After all, I am my father's daughter.

I constantly ask Dad to give me a sign from the other side. Although there have been many, the following is quite remarkable. A song, or parts of it, came in a dream one night. The following day I looked online to what I remembered, and found the song. One day later, sitting in the audience in Stratford, I listened to that song in Carousel. I believe, as in the storyline of the play, that my father came to earth for a day and made himself known to his daughter…me.

> *When you walk through a storm*
> *Hold your head up high*
> *And don't be afraid of the dark*
> *At the end of the storm*
> *There's a golden sky*
> *And the sweet silver song of a lark*
> *You'll Never Walk Alone, Carousel,*
> *Rogers & Hammerstein, 1945*

On Machu Picchu, over 14,000 feet above sea level, under the sky with the golden light of the sun, and in that space of sacredness, I meditated, prayed, and asked for a message. I left knowing I had come and accomplished more than I ever dreamed of. On the bus down the treacherous snake road from the top, I saw my message: a sign that spoke directly to my heart and soul, like a direct communication from God. Between two mountains was the most magnificent rainbow. Embracing the beauty of nature, I was filled to the brim with awe and luv. I remembered God's covenant with Noah in Genesis 9:12-16 that he would never again destroy the world. This rainbow meant more.

This was a symbol of hope, of blessings, following the right path, and of dreams come true and the promise of more being fulfilled.

My Sunshine, aka Sunnee, knew when Dad passed on, as she threw herself at a gate in the kitchen, moments before the phone rang. All the brown spots on her belly vanished. Had she seen Dad? Somehow she knew to come into that room that February evening. When I think of this I think of the book, *Dogs That Know When Their Owners Are Coming Home*, written by Rupert Sheldrake.

I read books, listened to teleseminars and took courses. I came across the TESOL (Teaching English as an Official Language) course and got my certificate of completion. Next was the Passionate Life Secrets course, from the authors Janet Bray Attwood and Chris Attwood of *The Passion Test*. I uncovered what my key passions are. By the way, number five was to become an author! At that time, I didn't understand why I was so passionate about becoming an author, but now it is clear. I have a story.

> *There is no greater agony than bearing an untold story inside you. A bird doesn't sing because it has an answer, it sings because it has a song.*
> *Maya Angelou, I Know Why the Caged Bird Sings*

I not only stoked the embers of my fire, but added new wood to make my fire stronger, bigger and brighter. I took more online courses, achieving my certificates as Law of Attraction Basic Practitioner, Basic Hypnotic Communicator, Ericksonian Hypnotist, NLP Practitioner, Life Coach, Master Life Coach, Coach in Life Optimization, and Coach Practitioner. I continue to feed this thirst for learning, managing the many programs and events in my life. Inspiring books and access to music are available in most rooms of my home. I have a deep appreciation for arts and culture, attending theatre, opera, lectures, fundraisers, galas, comedy, sports, concerts and more. I've had the privilege of hearing wisdom from visionaries and inspiring people. I will continue to serve humanity, sharing my experiences and the knowledge I have garnered to help others live their life of passion.

Life is a work of art, and I have a new canvas. With my tools and life as my classroom, anything is possible. Since this rose has bloomed, I embrace life and what it has in store for me.

> *Baby,*
> *I compare you to a kiss from a rose on the gray.*
> *Ooh,*
> *The more I get of you,*
> *The stranger it feels, yeah*
> *And now that your rose is in bloom.*
> *A light hits the gloom on the gray.*
> *Kiss From A Rose, Seal, 1987*

Luv is everything. Marci Shimoff says, "self-love is fundamental to our happiness." Luving yourself is the essence of your life, because when luv is present in your life, when it lives in you, there is peace. I show myself luv by making better choices. When you have self-luv, you are connected with the theme song of your life, and are living your purpose. Luving yourself is the key, the main theme of my chapter, and the message I wish to convey.

> *I believe in love, it's all we got*
> *Love has no boundaries, costs nothing to touch*
> *I Believe in Love, Elton John, 1996*

At a spa with my youngest daughter, her boyfriend and my husband, we sat in the hot tub outside. Flurries came down upon our heads. I stuck my tongue out to catch some! I was comforted knowing our fur babies at home were looked after. I climbed the stairs to look out over the beautiful landscape, so white and pure. I felt gratitude for my husband as he gives me the space I need that allows me to grow. I thought of my eldest daughter, recently married, now living her life of passion with her own menagerie of animals, expressing herself in the unique way she always has. I thought of my middle daughter, who will be married by the time this is in print, and how she constantly amazes me with her organizational skills, creativity, determination, and strength of conviction. My youngest daughter lives her life fully, and is already a published author. I am so proud of my daughters who live with values I worked hard to instill in them, each blossoming in their own way. I see myself in them, and that gives me an inner smile, knowing I also see so much of Mom in me. I thought of Mom and how we are lucky to be celebrating her 95th birthday. My stepdaughters, my sister and her family are all thriving. My friends take pleasure in their children who have grown into adulthood, as I do. I looked to the sky knowing at that moment Dad was looking down smiling.

> *If I had a box just for wishes*
> *And dreams that had never come true*
> *The box would be empty*
> *Except for the memory*
> *Of how they were answered by you*
>> *Time in a Bottle, Jim Croce, 1972*

By sharing my story, my *luv song*, I can inspire with a new knowledge. Perhaps everything I have gone through has brought me to this point in order to send a clear message—defeat didn't win—I am the victor! With the themes of your life, and tuning into your *luv song*, it *is* possible to find the journey home.

I am the author of my own life story. I intend on making it a good one. I am determined not to die with any of it left in me; rather, like a radio, I choose to turn up the dial in order to let the joy, peace and abundance of my luv song expand. In a place of luv, peace and gratitude, and connected to and with my heart, I have faith knowing that whatever is the next chapter of my life, it will bring me further toward my destiny.

> *Homeward bound*
> *Home where my thought's escaping*
> *Home where my music's playing*
> *Home where my love lies waiting*
> *Silently for me*
>> *Homeward Bound, Simon & Garfunkel, 1966*

DEATH AND DIVORCE: HEALING BY HELPING

Minni Sharma

My story is not unusual as we all will eventually experience the death of a loved one and almost half of us will divorce, but my journey is unique.

I have tried to take the crisis and traumatic events in my life and make it my life's work to help others. That is how I have healed. No matter what challenges I've been through in my life so far, I've come out even better, not just okay.

I achieved my university degree, got a government job and then got married—all by the age of 23.

In January of 1999 we found out that we were expecting our first baby. We were overjoyed. We couldn't wait to share the news with our families. This would be the first grandchild on either side of the family. I'll never forget the tears of joy my mother had when she finally realized that she was going to be a grandmother. I was fortunate enough to live with my parents in the first trimester of my pregnancy while our new house was being built. I recall one night in particular; I was about two months pregnant and vomiting at four in the morning when my mother came to the washroom to rub my back. I felt so tired and frustrated as I wasn't able to hold any food down and felt nauseous all the time. She whispered in my ear that this was a good sign, the baby was growing. She'd then go on to remind me that when she was pregnant with me, she was hospitalized for much of the pregnancy due to dehydration from vomiting so much, so I shouldn't really be complaining as much. I was so grateful and happy to have my mother's love, reassurance and guidance. She made everything okay.

My mother and I made so many plans in that time; the baby shower, an Indian ceremony to welcome the baby, religious ceremonies, the clothes and toys that we would buy. We watched the ultrasound video with such joy and anticipation of the arrival of the first grandson. In the Indian culture, usually the daughter moves into her mother's home temporarily after she has had the baby or the mother moves into the daughter's home to help out. Mom was going to take a few months off of work or even retire early so that she could spend time and help out with the baby. I picked the obstetrician that she liked and the hospital that was closer to her so that she could take a taxi over as soon as I went into labour. We talked every day and became closer than ever.

On June 21, 1999, my mother died tragically. She was crossing the street when a 91-year-old driver ran a red light and hit her. I was five and a half months pregnant and my mother was only 51 years old. She had a head and leg injury and after 10 days in the hospital, she succumbed to them.

I remember walking into the hospital that dreadful night. I had visited my mother at the hospital that morning and was confused as to why my husband was taking me downtown to see her again that evening and had no further information. I knew she had some injuries and short-term memory loss, but she was going to be ok as far as I knew.

When we arrived, I saw my cousins and other family members in the distance. They quickly walked away to avoid me. My father walked towards me in the hallway with an expressionless look. Then he quietly told me that Mom was now in a better place. I felt shocked. Family members ran towards me to catch me before I could fall to the ground.

I was the last person to find out that my mother had died. Everyone was afraid that the shock and grief may affect my pregnancy and the baby directly. I cried. Then I was asked if I wanted to see my mom and I said yes. Sometimes I wish I hadn't because that is not how I wanted to remember her. I said goodbye to her and I promised to take care of my father, brother and especially the baby. That was the first time I felt the baby kick. He was moving so much as if to let me know that he was grieving as well.

I remember wanting to blame someone for this tragedy. I did call the 91-year-old driver once and confronted him with not offering condolences or even flowers. I told him that he took away many years from my mother's life, that my son would never know his grandmother. All he could say to me was, "it was ordained to happen." I realized at that moment that I was not going to get a heartfelt apology from him. It was also my first real lesson in forgiveness. I rationalized that this man did not intend to wake up that morning to cause the death of my mother. I forgave him, let it go and never looked back after that conversation. I accepted that nothing would bring my mother back and I needed to focus on healing my pain and taking care of my baby.

Several months after my mother's death, I was at a family event where a few young moms were chatting about their experiences. One of them began talking about how grateful she was that her mother brought food over daily and took care of the baby whenever she and her husband wanted to go out. I immediately felt a gut-wrenching pit in my stomach at that moment and felt so hurt and resentful. I was forcing myself to hold back the tears. They looked at me and quickly changed the topic. I detested the looks of pity. I wanted to be seen as the happy new mom, not the poor girl whose mother died in a tragic accident while I was pregnant. I was in the depths of grief in those moments and was angry at the universe for taking this experience away from me, my mother and my children. Mom had never been happier in her life than when she was about to be a grandmother.

I miss her so much.

After my adorable son was born, I indulged everything into loving and caring for him. I put my grief aside for a while; still, I needed to heal. The grief affected my happiness, my health and even my relationships. I went to bereavement support groups and felt comforted by the others there who "got it." They understood the pain and did not judge me or my tears. I went to many years of therapy to learn skills and have tools to make me a stronger person. It was after that I decided to help others who were experiencing grief and loss. I did not go back to work after my son was born, I started to take courses and training to facilitate grief support groups. I loved it. I volunteered at a local hospice and supported women whose mothers had died. I felt a deep sense of peace and satisfaction that I may have helped another person heal and feel like they were not alone on their grief journey. I also took training and became a volunteer crisis counsellor for a rape crisis centre.

In fact, I took this even one huge step further and went back to school to do training in psychotherapy. This was my lifelong dream.

I still feel that my mother guides me when I need her most. I look for signs. When I was trying to make the decision about whether to continue my education and become a psychotherapist, I would drive in my car talking out loud to my mom. Right after I asked her if I should do it and to give me a sign, I saw a huge Nike billboard that said, "just do it." It may have been a coincidence but I saw it as a sign of support from my mother.

In 2003 my gorgeous daughter was born. We now had a million-dollar family. Our family was complete. Over time though, our marriage had become very emotionally toxic and I did not know how to make it better. There were such extreme emotions and incidents that I did not know how to handle. I tried everything to make my marriage work but felt so degraded and lost myself in the process.

Five years later, my husband and I separated and my family was torn apart. I felt powerless to stop it. I was so sad for my children who were only four and eight years old at the time. I felt shame and disappointment as divorce was still taboo in my cultural community and also in my eyes, personally. I felt like I had failed. At the same time though I felt a huge feeling of relief that I was no longer in an unhealthy relationship. I had been a stay-at-home mom for 10 years, had two beautiful children and no paying job. My self-esteem was at an all-time low. In my marriage I felt put down, especially for my weight gain. I was later diagnosed with hypothyroidism, which explained a lot!

At the time of my divorce, I was scared. How was I going to survive financially? How were my children going to get through this? Was I going to be alone forever? Questions filled my brain and my heart. I was very concerned for my children as they were my world. I had no idea that the next few years would be some of the most difficult. They would not, however, be without glimpses of hope and renewed faith.

I experienced a tumultuous divorce with many court appearances. Litigation sucked the life from me. It was all so unnecessary and sad. I did not want to fight. Despite concerns I had, I have always encouraged my children to have a peaceful relationship with their father. I watched my children being torn emotionally through this divorce, speaking to professional after professional. I felt as if the system had failed my children. I was so stressed out. I developed cluster headaches, also known as the suicide disease. I was on an oxygen tank every night for months at a time to try to relieve the excruciating pain, but nothing helped. I hid it from my children and my family. I put on a strong face but cried at night for my children who were devastated.

At the same time as I was going through my divorce, I was also supporting women through the family law court process while working at a women's shelter. I was engulfed by divorce both professionally and personally. It was awful, but it helped me to support women through this difficult time. I had seen many different outcomes and knew that family law was not as black and white as I had thought.

There were so many unethical and unjust events that occurred throughout my divorce. Never in a million years did I think I would be taken to court to prevent my children from living with me. I dedicated everything to taking care of my two children and was admired by friends and family as being an outstanding mother. My children meant and still mean everything to me.

Here I was at another court appearance where the lawyer on the other side made arguments that, if successful, would take our children's primary residence away from me and not allow me to move with my children, even though I was being forced out of the matrimonial home within a few weeks.

This was done, unfortunately, with the help of a parent coordinator, whom we had hired to help us with decisions regarding our children. She wrote a reporting letter to help support my ex-husband's position in court. I was horrified and extremely disappointed that a professional would conduct herself in such an unethical manner. The letter was riddled with hearsay and was completely biased and untrue. As I sat in court on that dreaded day while the senior judge in the Ontario Supreme court made her ruling, I was crippled by fear. This decision would alter my children's future for the worse, in my opinion, all based on this 'report' written by a professional involved in our case. The judge did not even hear the arguments that my lawyer had prepared as she had read the arguments and evidence on both sides prior to entering the courtroom.

There was a long, stale silence in the room as the judge started writing for what seemed like an eternity. I felt sick to my stomach and then finally the judge started to speak. I could not hear her words as they seemed to come out in slow motion and too distorted for my foggy brain to make out. I was unable to comprehend anything. My lawyer then whispered to me, "this is good." I immediately felt a huge weight lifted off my shoulders. Relief and joy overcame me as I held back the tears of happiness. I looked over at my partner and co-workers who were there to support me and saw their smiles. At that moment, I knew everything was going to be okay. The judge saw right through the unethical behavior of the professional involved and the opposing arguments and wrote quite a scathing report, I must say. I am so grateful that despite the horrendous situation, justice was served and the best interests of our children were put forth. We actually made case law! In other words, our case is used in family court as a reference when it comes to the role and responsibilities of a parent coordinator. I now feel that although it was a challenging situation, I have at least contributed to helping other families avoid a similar immoral situation.

While I was going through my divorce, I also did experience hope. I had met and fallen in love with a man who stood by me and supported me through this hell of a divorce. He was a positive influence for my children as well. I got a part-time job at a hospice as a bereavement coordinator, managed a rape crisis centre and worked at a women's shelter supporting women who were going through the same type of divorce that I was going through.

I was grateful to be employed. I was grateful to have found love. I was grateful that I could provide unconditional love to my children. I was grateful to see that my children were thriving, despite the volatility. I was also grateful I had always volunteered in my local community, which helped me gain employment after many years out of the workplace.

I have spent years in therapy, not wanting to tell my story over and over again, but to gain tools and skills to help me in times of adversity. I was finally able to feel empowered and confident again.

I now run my private practice as a psychotherapist in much the same manner. I tend to be solution-focused while assisting clients to heal their past, pain and patterns of behaviour. I see my job as helping guide people through their journeys—hence the name of my practice—*Guiding Journeys.*

I recently had an experience with a couple who came to me for divorce coaching. They could not agree on anything to do with their children as their anger and resentment towards each other took over. I hesitated to share my story but was so disappointed that they could not see what they were doing to their children that I shared a bit about my conflictual divorce. I explained that I did not want their children to go through what my children had. It was amazing to see the shift in their level of trust and comfort with me as a professional, and also in the way they viewed their conflict and how it was negatively impacting their family. They were finally able to see past the hurt and put their children's best interests first. I get it—not just the theory, but I've lived it. I try to help my clients put ego, power and control aside. I urge them to manage their mental health issues. I ask them to love their children more than they hate their ex. I don't really believe in involving the children professionally. I'd rather spend time and resources providing tools and skills to the parents to help them communicate through the difficult process of separation and divorce and thereafter. This makes for healthier, happier people. Most importantly, it is the best gift that anyone can give to their children!

I look at my son and daughter now and feel so proud of how they are becoming such wonderful and successful young adults. My son is a kind, compassionate young man. My daughter is beautiful, intelligent and carries an inner confidence. My children drive me to work harder and be a better person. They are proof that providing unconditional love and supporting our children does really work.

I value those days where I come home from working with clients who are managing their divorce in a healthy way with my guidance. I sit on my couch with a nice hot cup of tea. I look around and feel so grateful that I have a warm, safe home. I reflect on how fortunate I am to be of service to others and able to support individuals and families navigate divorce with dignity and respect, helping them make better decisions that are in the best interests of their children. I feel passionate about running workshops that empower women to communicate effectively, and to create healthy relationships and boundaries. Although I still struggle with my own fear and doubt at times, I now own my own home, a private practice and, perhaps most importantly, myself.

Of course, the very moment that I feel most relaxed, at peace and about to take my first sip of tea, my children walk through the door full of energy and wanting to share their day's events from school. Here starts the chaos of life again, but I love every minute of it. There's nothing more gratifying than knowing that I came out of these losses even better, not just okay.

TRUSTING GOD'S PLAN

Heather Gordon

Sitting in my cool dark salon with tears running down my tired face, it started to hit me: I made it! That sunny Saturday afternoon, after a busy week filled with making others feel their best, it was the first time it all sunk in. I felt the success and empowerment within.

Years prior, I certainly didn't feel that way—I remember my mom's words then, "you have always been my little gypsy." It was after I told my mom I wasn't coming home from my Vegas vacation, a time in my life where I needed clarity in my goals so I decided to stay, find myself and hash out some sort of life plan. It was there I found a part of myself I did not know existed, and a part that I actually admired.

I was 24 at the time. I had just finished college with a Bachelors of Science in Business Administration, along with the double major of logistics management, marketing and then cosmetology school. For some reason, after all of that, I was still not sure where to go from that point forward. I felt a void deep inside me, a longing for something more though I wasn't sure what it was at that time. My mom told me there will always be a void. It was something I refused to believe. I knew deep inside me there was something more.

We took weekend adventures during that time in Vegas that started to allow me to see a new vision and season rising in my life. One day, I found myself standing at the tip of Mount Zion, the most picturesque view of red rock and light gleaning across an expanse of landscape that seemed to go on for miles. I could feel the wind blowing around me and the sun shining down on me. It was breathtaking... It was exhilarating... It was hope-defined. The void within me was starting to fill with passion and a new thirst for life; this new-found hope was allowing me to begin to follow my dreams and be the best version of myself. It was everything I had been searching for, and opened for me what I didn't know would become some of the best adventures of my life.

It was there, at the tip of that mountain, that I made a monumental decision: I wanted to own a business, my very own hair salon. I wanted to be able to make women feel and look beautiful, every day.

I moved home from my adventures in Vegas and began. It was then I created HG Salon. I hired my first stylist to work for me and it was the greatest feeling to be a business owner. I saw my vision and goal, and it was starting to take shape and become reality.

My first employee, to this day, is still an amazing friend. She has been there with me through everything and for that I am truly grateful. Within the first week, I had enough money to pay rent for the month and from that day we have never looked back. It was not without hard work, focus and commitment to the point that I was working from seven in the morning until 10 at night, six or seven days a week.

Things were great, fast-moving, and my business was soaring, but all of the stress and emotion that goes with starting up and operating a business was starting to get to me. I kept telling myself to keep going. I had made it this far; I was not about to give up on my goal. I knew that if I persevered, I was not only making a future for myself, I was completely filling the hole in my core.

I decided to do the opposite of giving up and become a more specialized, educated stylist. Being young, being a woman, being an entrepreneur, and working in a small town, I needed to be respected to be established successfully. I worked hard and went on to become a national educator for Italy Hair Fashions, completed Aquage Master Class in Chicago, and became certified in Di Biase Hair Extensions USA, which led to becoming a USA Educator for Di Biase. It was at this extension certification class where I met Vikki and Dale, owners of Di Biase Hair Extensions USA. I was totally unaware of the process occurring at that time, however, this talented, successful and kind-hearted woman would become my professional mentor.

I truly believe that God has a plan and He puts people in your life for a reason. Vikki has mentored me to levels I never knew possible, showing me a world well outside of a small town. She pushes me to be my best, offering opportunities to fulfill my dreams, goals and really amplify my life. An opportunity I'll never forget is assisting at the Mrs. United States Pageant, all the glamour and empowerment and women shining at their best in Las Vegas, the same place where my sparkle of a dream and those early goals of becoming a business owner first were born. I reach new heights and continue to learn from Vikki and so many in my life.

My family is also a huge factor in my success; their work ethic in life, the challenges they've faced and overcome, each family member my mentor along the way. My family is the main anchor in my life. They are there for me 100 percent even if they do not agree with me 100 percent. They have loaded up a horse trailer more than once to move me where the wind blows. My heart fills with happiness and love and warmth when I think of them; they are beautiful people, farmers from a rural small town, where agriculture drives the economy, and they are lovers of life.

Farming has its own work ethic; hard physical labour, endurance, perseverance, and above all, a faith that goes beyond the day-to-day. This has been imprinted on my soul; my story connects with this simple, yet complicated, principle. We are all a product of how and where we grow up, whether it's on a conscious or subconscious level.

My family's imprint reaches far beyond work ethic too. Everyone's life is influenced by one or more sentinel events; mine were living through life-altering events that I know gave me wisdom, fortitude and confidence to pursue my dreams of owning my hair salon business and becoming well-known in the hair industry.

My dad's health was that first sentinel event. In 1990, my twin sister Heidi and I were in our room during our nightly story time, our dad telling us snowmobile stories to get us to sleep. He always dozed off before we did; it was a particular night though I remember clearly, and has motivated me to keep going and live life to its fullest. That night while laying in my bed, my father suffered a brain aneurism.

He spent months in the hospital; I remember my worry and concern. We were such a close-knit family and this experience was the first major one that not only separated us physically, but frightened us so much because we didn't know exactly what was going on. I felt like my dad was ripped from me, and I couldn't see him for the longest time.

I remember thinking, I need to trust God, and that's what I did. I am so grateful my dad pulled through. My mom was so strong then, too. I admired her and continue to, to this day, for her strength, kindness, and faith.

The second sentinel event involved my brother when I was in high school. He was diagnosed with cancer. My brother and mom spent two months in Detroit, two hours from our home, battling this monster. He had two stem cell transplants. The first was with his own cells and when that didn't work then it was a transplant from a donor in Germany.

My mom was the pillar of support once again. As with my dad, she tried to soften the truth from us. When we visited, I remember the pale, lifeless look of my brother, struggling for life. My mom promised him everything and anything if he lived. The support from our community was overwhelming. A spaghetti dinner was organized to raise money for testing to find a bone marrow donor. Heidi and I were not a match to my brother, only to each other. The people in attendance and the money raised was phenomenal; over $20,000 and hundreds of people tested.

None of them were matches to my brother, however, since then a good number were a match to others all over the United States. For us, we had to keep our faith, and it was strong. A match came in from across the world and it amazed me how everyone is connected in one way or another. The world is still a small place and God has a plan.

During this whole experience, my family and I felt broken, but in the end, we became stronger. My brother is an inspiration in our family and during that ordeal I realized that if he can keep on fighting through all of this, then I can thrive when the going gets tough. If he can rally from this speed bump in life, I can come back from anything. I needed to continue to have faith and trust in God's plan and for some time I was able to do that.

God's plan is what led me to start my business, however, after five years of waking up early, going to bed late, skipping vacations when everyone else enjoyed these life experiences, being married to my business rather than my husband, and having my priorities all messed up, I could feel the burnout creeping in.

The thought of giving up began to build in my brain every day. It was when I thought I had it all that my world came crashing down.

Eventually, everything I worked so hard for did not seem to matter; I felt like it had no purpose. Three of my top hair designers suddenly left the salon, which set me back not only on the business side but it took its toll on me as a leader. It left me searching for answers of why, and made me reevaluate my core values, my leadership skills, my entire business plan. I worked so hard to build to be successful. The top stylist was leaving at that time and it felt like a slap in the face.

Where is the loyalty? I give and give and motivate and show kindness and where did it get me?

My personal life was crumbling, too. I was in the process of divorcing my then-husband. I strive to help so many and empower women, yet I felt I didn't exist in the relationship. How could I find the power or inner strength to stand up for myself when that man is supposed to be my everything?

I own a large and successful salon. To the outside world, I had everything. How could I feel so lonely inside, so lost and torn? How could I feel so worthless and unimportant? I know deep down the man I called my husband loved me. I know he wanted a family and a life together and I know that he wouldn't have been satisfied or fulfilled. How could I also make him feel this way? How could I give more to my business than to the man I loved? It wasn't fair to either of us. I thought that all the tears, anger and emotion I went through would have to make sense eventually. Sixteen months later though I still hadn't found the peace I had been looking for. I felt like a prisoner in my life. It honestly was one of the hardest decisions to make, but I kept telling myself, I need to trust God's plan.

As much pain and as many mixed emotions as I was experiencing, I had to take deep breaths and force myself to just keep moving, endure and persevere. Now I realize that to truly be successful you have to have your priorities straight. It was too late for my marriage; it was time to move on and take ownership of my life and be the empowered woman I know I am.

Feeling unappreciated personally and professionally, I knew my game plan and approach had to change. I had been so preoccupied in lifting the salon to success that I did not make time to really focus on myself, or where and what I wanted the salon to truly be.

To give to myself and pick myself back up from the ground, I decided to hire a consultant and an administrative assistant to help me reach my goals. These two women, along with the other stylists in the salon, have made a world of a difference. I had been physically and mentally exhausted through this whole process, but instead of being exhausted like a hamster spinning in her wheel, I am now like a soaring bird, high above the land. In the same week as I am bustling along on a warm November day while everyone is getting ready for their holiday parties, a business student in college and a cosmetology student both requested an interview with me about mentorship. Me, a mentor! From a renewed place, I could be giving back!

As the cosmetology student asks me questions about my mentors and influential people in my life, I think back to all the guidance I was given and how good it makes me feel to share that and pass it on. As I spoke, I felt it within: I am a strong, independent woman for these young women to look up to. It was one of those 'a-ha' moments. The college student was asking me about leadership in the workplace and managing people. Years ago, I would never have imagined myself managing people, guiding people or being a strong public figure.

I started to find my "happy place" and that void once again began to fill. It is the place where I can be creative, hard-working, even strategic, and empowering. I can help others find goals and aspirations. This place allows me to be myself and feel good. I love touching so many hearts in one day. I love the warmth and support of my clients and team. I love the opportunity to always learn and be better. I will never forget one of my veteran stylists saying that she has never had a boss that motivated her to be a better person as I had. That to me is the best compliment. I want to motivate others to do all they can achieve; to be their best, to have goals and dreams, to know that they can reach that star.

I now know too that going for your dreams comes with balancing the joys of life. In the challenges of being a business owner, I had lost sight of the important things in life. It was not until my life came crashing down that I realized what truly is important. To be successful, you need to learn to take time for yourself and your family. You need to learn how to balance work and play.

I spent five years of my life working so hard that I did not take the time to be with my friends or family. It was during this time that my twin sister had her first child, my first nephew. I wanted to spend more time with this incredible little boy, but I was pressured to focus on my business. In a very subtle way, I became my own worst enemy. This was the path to my eventual burnout, and a defeatist attitude to put an end to all of my goals. One of the hardest parts of my life was to figure out who I truly am, to reevaluate everything, because giving up is so easy. Pushing toward the wrong door is exhausting—it is said that the definition of insanity is doing things the same way and expecting a different result. So I needed to redefine my life and trust in God's plan. The key I found is listening to what that plan is.

It took a tremendous amount of work, perseverance, sheer sweat-equity, endurance, faith and a rollercoaster of emotions to get me where I am today, but here I am. Gratification fills my heart knowing the salon has won numerous awards: Sanilac County The Best of the Best 2014, Silver Lining Business Award 2012, The Croswell-Lexington Chamber of Commerce Business Spirit Award 2012, and Croswell's Swinging Bridge Festival Mayor's Award 2010/2015. As a young woman entrepreneur, I have touched so many lives and helped so many hearts. I'm truly proud of all of my hard work and the way things have turned out. I listened to my needs and trusted God's plan.

A gypsy at heart and an empowering woman entrepreneur.

Now, living a life not only with trust and faith, but with balance. Sitting in my salon chair reminiscing about my hardships and successes, I am interrupted by little feet coming from the back door. These little feet are my nephew and niece that I am taking to the park to enjoy the sun, get fresh air and enjoy life. My heart is happy. Happiness is truly the key to success. I had to hit rock bottom, and become a different kind of person and leader, to truly make me realize what it means to be successful. It is something every young woman can do no matter what your background is or where you are from. Always remember where you come from yet never forget the sky's the limit and keep shooting for your goals.

With hard work and the desire to want more, you can be whoever you want to be and make it your mission to fill that missing piece of your core. I challenge all of you to love big, dream big, and above all, be authentic. Go out in the world and make a difference while enjoying your life on the way. Do not let anyone stop you. Do not give up along the way because you have come so far to stop following your dreams. Make sure you remember to keep on keepin' on!

SHARING MY GIFT

Lisa Rizzo

I am standing in a room of 30 people. There are a hundred spirits here, too, all wanting to be heard. The energy, its intensity—sometimes I have to step back and take a break. I want to give details of what I see, feel and know. The spirits are there with purpose, sharing what they need to; whether it's to move on, say sorry or validate themselves, they are there for a reason and I'm there to relay it for them.

The energy in the room is palpable. Every spirit wanting a voice through me. I see a woman in the second row in tears. Her mom's presence is here. "She passed away from something in her chest," I said. She nods. Her mother's spirit wants her daughter to know how much she loves her. "She wants you to let go of the hurt and pain," I tell her. "She says she is with you every day." Tears of joy stream down the woman's face.

My calling, my purpose, is to help my Creator and his angels assist settled souls in this realm to move on and make peace. I also help those here on earth fear less and love more…

Even before I was five years old, my spirit wanted to help people. Around that time, I noticed changes in myself. I started to see glimmers, shadows of people I knew were not of this world. They spoke to me, asking me to help them. I didn't understand then; I would sit in my room and talk to the shadows and voices, their comfort strong. Even without knowing how I could help, I felt ease, not fear, with these spirits.

There were also many changes going on in my mother. She became depressed and abusive, completely disconnected from reality. She didn't know how to show me love as a young child; no affection, no kind words. I loved my mother though and knew I wanted to help her.

One night my mother was watching TV while I was colouring. I turned my head and saw the figure of an angel walking by us. I looked at my mother. "Did you see that angel walk by?" I asked. My mother, with a glazed look in her eyes, said, "that's just your imagination." I was seven years old at this point, so I trusted my mother's judgment; it must have been my imagination.

Later on, my mother would walk in a room where I was talking to someone who was not there visually, at least for her. She would yell at me and tell me to stop. It made her very uncomfortable. For me though, I felt loved and safe, my senses enhanced and nurtured in a positive way. It was like I knew I am here to live this earthbound plane, and was being trained to serve others from here on earth and beyond.

I always felt very different from everyone else in my family. I remember one night vividly. I woke and walked to my mother's bedroom; standing over her, I watched as her spirit left her body. I must've been around 9 years old. I wasn't frightened, I was fascinated and knew my spirit guides were showing me things I needed to see, hear, feel, smell and touch. I stood there for what felt like minutes; it was actually hours. Then suddenly, I watched as my mother's spirit descended, back into her body, vanishing into her. My mother woke with a start—"what are you doing?" she asked. "Watching your spirit return to your body," I said. "Go back to bed," she said.

At 10 years old, I spent days on the balcony porch two stories high in my apartment complex, writing songs and singing my heart out. One particular day, I went to the front porch and rain was showering down. Like any other day, I looked to the sky, and started to sing. "Look down," I heard, "to the street." It was my spirit guides. They were always putting things in front of me I needed to know and learn. There I saw seven or eight people, watching me. "Sing more, sing more," they said, clapping their hands.

I didn't know then I was already helping people. They were spirits; I was bringing them comfort, too. There are those who walk among us, those who have passed and those who have not yet passed to the other side. There they were, feeling joy in listening to a 10-year-old girl sing.

At 10, I was already helping people on the other side to move on. I could also see things before they would happen, my spirit guides sharing with me events before they took place. I was learning trust; they were teaching me not to fear the challenges of what they put on my path.

This is my gift. I knew then I had something special within. That day, raindrops showering me as I sang, I knew what to do with my gift. I had to share it with the people, the spirits, who came to me for help.

At 13, I stopped talking to my mother about my visions. "People will think you're crazy," she'd snarl at me, "you've got to stop talking like that." So I stopped telling her about everything. I needed to understand though, and to help others. One Sunday morning, I told my mom I was going to church. She looked at me completely bewildered. I was going because I needed answers to my questions; I told her I needed to find my religion, what I believe in.

I walked an hour to the church on that hot summer day. I sat down in the pew, looking around, waiting for answers. Then I saw them: both spirit guides standing strong beside me.

"You have been through so much already. You will go through so much more," they said. *Well that's not fair, why me?* I thought. *That makes no sense!* I left the church feeling confused. I cried myself to sleep that night, feeling like I couldn't talk to a single soul about what was going on with me.

I then started reading a lot of books on spirituality. There wasn't a big selection at the library, but I felt great comfort in reading and getting some understanding, learning it was okay to embrace my calling.

By 18, I had been through physical, mental and sexual abuse, and was also a victim of date rape. It was like I was born into a world that tried to break my spirit from the day I entered it. At the same time, I was given a gift; at that age, I still didn't understand it. I was angry and confused, not knowing what it felt like to be loved, still I was always willing to overcome struggles and fight for something within me.

I know you may be asking, why would my spirit guides let me experience so much pain? I always knew our guides cannot control what happens in this world; everything we experience, good or bad, has its purpose. It is a lesson learned, and has a greater meaning for our spirits to overcome and shine when we return home to the other side.

At 18 years old, my story and life changed. I sat on the front porch one night, gazing at the stars, asking the universe, *where do I go from here?* In the same breath, I longed for more. Resonant, clear, I heard a voice whisper in my ear, *ask for what you want and live it every day.*

It was a lightning bolt a-ha moment. I had never asked for anything. I gazed to the stars again. "Please," I said, "send me someone to love and accept me for all I am, and all I will become, my protector."

I nuzzled into bed that night, feeling great peace while asleep. I awoke and felt happy inside, something new, an aliveness that radiated my entire being. I went to work that day and couldn't wait for my shift to end, as though I had plans that night, even though I didn't. I went home, took a shower, got dressed and did my makeup. Just as I sat on my front porch, my friend showed up—"let's do something different tonight," she said. "You know what," I said, "I think we should. Let's fill up the car and just drive. Wherever we end up, we end up."

We hopped in her car and rode on the 104 highway, Rochester, U.S., to Toronto, Canada. We thought it was the coolest thing, two 18-year-olds in a different country, going to hang out in the big city.

The city was bustling; I had never seen such a busy place in my life. Cars everywhere, and so many people. We started driving on Yonge Street, the longest street in the world, looking for a place to stay. It was overwhelming and exciting. We were having a hard time finding a hotel, everything was booked. We saw a group of guys walking by and asked them if they knew anywhere to stay in Toronto. One of the guys came up to the car and asked if we want to hang out and grab a slice of pizza. They would also help us find a place to stay.

I immediately connected with one of the guys, Carlo. I felt really comfortable around him; yet at the same time, I didn't trust and didn't want to put myself out there at all. It ended up being a fun night, and they did help us find a hotel close by.

The next morning, there was a knock on our hotel room door. My girlfriend looked through the peephole. "It's Carlo," she said, "and his friend." She opened the door and the guys asked us if we wanted to hang out again that day. "Sure," we said, as we didn't have to work again until the next day.

As I was getting ready in the bathroom, I caught Carlo's glances at me in the mirror. I continued putting my makeup on, feeling his eyes on me. My spirit guide whispered, "turn to him." When I spun around, he realized I knew he was watching me. I don't know what made me do what I did next, but I walked over to him and planted a kiss right on him. Yes, it was a guy I had just met, but I always follow my intuition, it has never failed me.

The rest of the day, we adventured around Toronto, sightseeing. Carlo and I were inseparable, holding hands, kissing and talking about life as if we had known each other forever. By the end of the day, we knew one thing for sure: how we felt around one another, and that we wanted to continue to feel that way. We had no idea how we would make the relationship work, but we went for it, writing each other, talking on the phone and I would drive to Toronto every other weekend, working two jobs to make sure I had enough money to cover all my expenses.

I was living the life of an adult. I was also taking care of my mother, but for the first time in my life I had something to look forward to, seeing Carlo as much as I could. I felt so good around him; he made me feel safe. He didn't know what I was going through back home and, to be honest, I didn't want to share it with him, not yet. I just wanted to enjoy the feeling within myself that was growing. I knew my guides put him in my path for a reason.

Everyone told us, "there's no way your relationship will last." Carlo and I didn't worry about whether we would make it; we wanted to enjoy the ride. We knew we were soulmates.

At 20 years old, I became pregnant. I was living in Rochester and Carlo was living in Canada. I was scared to death when I found out. Taking care of myself and my mother was already so much for me, and the last thing I wanted was to take from Carlo's youth with him raising a child. I called him after my doctor's appointment. I was crying, and told him I was pregnant.

I never heard a man so happy in my life! It was not how I expected him to react. He packed everything then and there, leaving his parents a note saying he was moving to Rochester to be with me and his baby. We had three hundred dollars in our pockets, not a clue where to live or how we would put food on the table. We did know one thing: how much we loved each other, and that it would all work out. Six months after our son was born, I married the man of my dreams.

As I got older, my five senses heightened. Touch, taste, smell, sight and sound—they all intensified so deeply. Being in a room with 10 people became like being in a room with 50. Spirits come to me often, especially when I have those gathered who want help or deep peace. It is something my spirit guides taught me from a young age: I must separate the living and the dead that walk alongside us, and be the link to facilitate greater healing.

In a way, it's like life among the living. There are good people and bad, and all kinds of energies. The only reason the gifted are unique is they have no fear. Humans, much of the time, fear what they cannot see or feel. We move with the universe though, a greater purpose the current of our lives. You were not sent here to suffer, instead to learn and observe and nurture the purpose of your soul.

The good, the bad, darkness and light, pervade all areas of life. The darkness is all things unholy, souls chosen to serve the devil, or the many names he is called by followers here on earth and beyond. The only way his followers or creations walk among the living is by feeding on souls that are weak, ones easily possessed and drained of energy.

I have recently encountered the darkness; you must know that in my spirit, I am a warrior! When dealing with something not of this world, I fiercely fight it to send it back where it came from because I have no fear.

It was a day my daughter came home with a serious headache. Within minutes my husband, my youngest son and I started to feel a headache too. I knew right away, something dark had attached itself to my daughter's spirit. I needed to cleanse with saging, and call out to my Native ancestors' mother for guidance. I called to her and she said, "you must share this experience with your daughter." It was not what I wanted to hear—I feared my daughter couldn't handle it. Then I quickly came back to my centre, my guides clearly telling me the word fear was not acceptable.

I explained this to my daughter, and at first, she was scared, but she knew and trusted that I would never put her in harm's way. We started in the basement, working up to the top floor. In each room, we turned on each light, using sage to cleanse and push the dark spirits away. As we walked from each room, we shut the lights and the door so the sage could do its work, clearing the negative energy.

I blew sage from a shell, and my daughter walked behind me. We could feel the heaviness, darkness all around us. In a moment the dark spirit blew sage in my face, and my hair was on fire!

"Do not show it fear," I told my daughter, and she didn't. We continued saging and suddenly my neck caught fire too. My daughter said, "Mom, just push through," and I did.

In the last room we were saging, my daughter closed her eyes, our dog was howling and I was not me. A dark spirit had attached itself to me. It was not leaving without a fight, so that is what I gave it.

My daughter looked at me, brave. "Mom, I have all the faith in the world you can handle this." She could feel its energy, waiting for her to crumble. She did not. I sent that dark spirit back to its world.

Afterwards, the house felt so much lighter. I was so proud of my daughter for her powerful positive spirit and the trust she gave me to help her with something she couldn't see with her own eyes.

Just then, my daughter asked if she could take a picture of my neck. "Sure," I said, and she took a picture to show me. Scratches ran the length of my neck; my daughter had witnessed them happening right in front of her eyes.

~~~

Connecting as a spiritual Medium is something that permeates every aspect of my life. I own two businesses, a franchise and a plumbing company. You might wonder how a spiritual Medium manages day-to-day life while walking alongside the dead. It has taken many years, as spirits connect with me every day. Just as you may ask the living to give you space or time for yourself, you hope the dead will respect your time and space as needed. With the dead though, we understand that spirits are coming to us for help and guidance so they can move forward with their journey. It can be hard for them when you're the only thing that can help them, or even see or hear them amidst the world of the living.

I remember one day as I went to open the door to my store, I saw a woman and the spirit of a young boy standing next to her. I know when I see a spirit as clear as you and I, it is taking all their energy to be that present with the living. I knew I had to send this woman a message.

"How do you feel about Mediums?" I asked her, and she looked at me, bewildered. "You have a young man standing beside you." The boy spirit told me he passed in a car accident. I then told her the make and colour of the car.

"How in the hell do you know all this?" she said.

"I'm a Medium."

The young man was her son, she told me. She had lost him a few years back.

"Your son says you still don't believe me he's here," I said, and she started to laugh. "That's okay," I said. "He wants me to give you this number, 27." She didn't know what the number 27 meant.

The next day I went to open the store and the woman ran inside, yelling, "I know what the 27 is!" It was the hockey jersey number she had buried her son in. I looked at her and said, "well I guess you believe it was him then." She started to cry and thanked me. Of course I was so happy for her to get her message.

When I offer people insight, it gives me great joy to see them at peace. Helping people receive closure and insight is something I look forward to every day. As with all the experiences that led me to where I am now—standing in a room full of people, both living and dead, and sharing messages needed for healing—I am so grateful for this gift. My life's focus is to do as much as possible with this gift I've been given. I accepted a long time ago these were the visions I have, my purpose.

Now, as tears roll down the woman's face when she hears her mother's message, I know this to be true. I see sighs of relief around the whole room, and feel the next message for the next person, each spirit guiding me to help bring them home. It's peace and healing for the living and the dead. I am the bridge, the voice, the link that connects with and shares the two.

The scene is captured by a brilliant camera crew, one moment of many portrayed in my web series, "The Link." When Stefano Pucciano, talented and innovative producer shared his vision, I knew the series was the next step on my path. I have known for many years how things would fall into place, my gift expanding and the ways in which I can share it, too. Radio, television, books—all media that allows me to help more people, bring more love and less fear. I knew I would have a web series, be on television and radio, be in a book, and that I would write a book of my own.

I knew I would be standing in this room of people, shooting my series, seeing tears of joy streaming down this woman's face. I see the collective exhale every time I share a message, give someone peace. It's peace for the living and the dead, my connection to both the link, and my gift to share so I do.

BREAKING FREE

Laura Vella

"Until lions start writing down their own stories,
tales of the hunt shall glorify the hunter"
~ African proverb

Ask and you shall receive.

Well, I asked, pleaded and begged. I received. They sent me the most beautiful angel who helped me break free...

It was February 5th, 2007, her name was Sandra Shaw. I had no idea what to expect—tarot cards, palm reading, maybe tea leaves. I went in with no expectations, yet little did I know how this one reading was about to change my life forever. I would finally receive the healing I had been praying for.

Sandra was not only a psychic, but was also a medium. I had never seen a medium before. Beginning with a prayer, she invites any spirits, guides or teachers to come forward who want to share any wisdom or knowledge they have to help you with whatever is in your heart and mind. Within seconds, a woman spirit appeared to Sandra, but

I could not see or hear her. The spirit was crying and so emotional, it took Sandra by surprise. She's from my mother's side of the family, the spirit revealed—"my poor baby, her innocence is gone, you don't know how she suffered and has carried this sadness." I was shocked, I wasn't expecting any of this. All I could think was, *wow, I'm not alone!*

"Something happened a long time ago," and it was hard for this lady spirit to talk about. Something that "stole my innocence away." Wow, she nailed it. I knew the exact moment she was referring to and burst into tears.

I knew he should not have been trying to get into the bathroom where I was taking a bath. I was just a little girl, around seven or eight years old. It was summer. The second I heard him rustling with the doorknob I knew I was in danger; he was going to hurt me! Within seconds the shower curtain opened, he knelt down. *No, no, no, this is not happening to me.* I scream in my mind. He leans for the bar of soap; I'm paralyzed, he begins to wash me. It's only been seconds since his break in but it feels like hours. He moves quickly and I know where he wants to go. My body cringes. That bar of soap glides quickly down my back, he has to move fast, his wife and my brother will be back any minute. He fondles my butt, I bolt upright. I felt my soul separate, float away. I'll never forget that moment. A piece of me dies, this was too much for my little soul. The feeling of violation as my body was invaded by this man, the man who I considered a second father. I'm betrayed in the worst possible way. I'm floating, I can't feel, I'm numb, not strong enough to endure any more. I know one thing; he's not going any further. I say nothing, my eyes do all the talking. I look him dead in the eyes. He knows I know what he wants, he knows I know what he has done is wrong and he knows I know what he wants to continue to do is wrong. The terror in my eyes saves me, that look I gave him saves me.

"You can't tell anyone this happened or I will get into a lot of trouble."

That was "our little secret"...

124

It wasn't until this moment with Sandra that anyone in my family had ever validated my traumas by this man. Even though I didn't know who this lady spirit was, there was a deep, deep bond. She feels my pain and refers to me as "her little one." I understand Sandra when she said, "she's more of a mother to me than my own mother," again, confirming what I knew since being a child—there was no mother-daughter bond ever with my mother.

"I have two men here in the room with us," Sandra continues. "Spirits don't usually do this, but they are showing me something very profound, I know the reason you are here. A grandfather is standing there." Oh my God, I know it's my Nonno! "Lora, you need me, you call me," the memory of his words ringing so loudly in my ears. He showed up for me! He apparently dragged this other grandfather spirit to show him, "look what you did to your family member, who in turn, hurt my family member." He was very angry. I completely understood what my Nonno was saying because I was well-educated on the subject of sexual abuse, understanding how it can be carried on generationally. For the first time in my life I'm being validated by somebody in my own family. Nonno knows the truth and I realize he was always with me, I was never alone. In all my days of suffering alone, abandoned and rejected by my family, my Nonno had always been with me!

They went on to show Sandra my suicide attempt...

"What's the matter with you, you look like someone died!" My mother caught me alone in that moment, out in the lounge area where my brother's engagement party was underway. Her tone, disgusted, like I was causing a problem for her. Again, as always, my emotions were a problem for her. The damage her words and actions caused me in this moment was surreal. Someone might as well have died, because I was surely feeling as though I was grieving a loss. You know what, I was—Laura was dead.

With unbearable sadness waking up that day, immediately I knew something was terribly wrong. I felt completely dead. No light in my eyes, no sparkle, no glimmer of hope. My eyes were black, vacant. The tears flowed endlessly, uncontrollably, all day, all night. I just needed my mother to step up, but would she ever be there for me? I felt so unworthy, useless, rejected.

I desperately needed a normal, nurturing mother, just this one time! After the continuous chances I gave her, the hope I had she would one day step up for me, her daughter. She saw my life in continuous despair, here was my darkest, lowest moment, here was her chance. Nope, instead, further rejection. That would not stop me, my fight to win her love would continue for years.

I overdosed that night on a bottle of painkillers. A lifetime of endlessly being rejected, I couldn't handle anymore, it was too much for my heart. I'd been fighting with my boyfriend at the time and let's just say he added further rejection. I didn't want to die, I just needed my mother to acknowledge me, my life, to make me important to her, to get us help I so desperately wanted for us. I loved my mom. "You have a choice to make a new choice," I'd say, but she always chose the same behavior, to reject and betray me. My mother hated me.

Having my stomach pumped was the worst experience of my life. By the grace of God, I didn't die or have liver damage.

My Nonno was my hero, my everything. My mother's father. He was the one I came to count on to be there for me, as he was always available to me, always, and he continuously let me know it. He drove me everywhere I needed to go, to and from school and work, to co-op, to my sporting practices and games, the mall, anywhere I needed to go. He always said, "Lora, you need me, you call me." And he meant it. I clung to those words. I needed to know someone had my back in life. I felt so special with my Nonno, he had my back. To me, the way someone showed me they loved and cared for me was through their actions, not words. Words were fluff. My dad was amazing, he provided everything I needed materially, but he was a workaholic and emotionally unavailable. As a young girl, I needed a solid, reliable, trusting male role model. I needed to know I could count on someone. Nonno was that someone.

Imagine how devastated I was when my hero, my Nonno, passed away unexpectedly within three weeks of being diagnosed with lung cancer. We had no idea he was even sick. He went into the hospital one day and never came out. Nothing was more devastating than seeing my Nonno dying in that hospital bed. His passing was the saddest day of my life, a piece of me died with him. I was 19. My hero was gone. Who would be there for me now?

"You hear me," my Nonno told Sandra.

I finally understood what he meant by that in the summer of 2011. Stripes my kitty is curled up next to me as I'm watching a movie on my laptop. A soft thump from my closet. We both jump, look over at it but I ignore it and go back to my movie. Thump, a couple seconds later, a tad louder this time. Again, we both jump, we look over at my closet, again, ignore. Thump! This third thump was so loud it scared the crap out of us! As I looked over to my closet, my heart racing, I finally realized I couldn't ignore this anymore, someone wanted my attention. But who? My hero, that's who! Within seconds I felt my Nonno's energy just wash completely over me. The connection in that moment was so beautiful, so powerful, so strong. I will never forget that moment. It was as if he was right there holding my hand. Everything suddenly made sense. All the knocks I had been hearing but ignoring since moving in a few months prior had been my Nonno all along, I was just scared to acknowledge them. Don't underestimate the spiritual world—they will do whatever they have to, to get our attention. In my case, my Nonno had to scare the crap out of me to finally get my attention!

~ ~ ~

"You've been giving me attitude all week." In the next breath, "I know what happened, your sister told me." It was a tone that implied she was upset with me, but why? I didn't do anything wrong. Once I tell her, she'll understand my "moodiness" and "attitude" I have been giving her.

This is where the profound emotional abandonment begins. I had just turned 21 years old. I had gone to visit my mom as I lived with my Nonna during this time. In her basement, it's just the two of us, face to face as we sat on the couch. I began from the beginning, divulging full details, of what this sick, perverted man subjected me to exactly one week prior. I was scared shitless. This was an uncomfortable conversation ahead but full honesty was needed, no sugar coating. She needs to know this man is sick, someone who is very close to her.

Every Monday he brought me out for lunch. We hung out all the time. The adults saw how much time he spent with me, never questioning him. I truly thought he cared about me. I was so desperate for a male figure in my life, I was just happy someone was paying attention to me. He was so invested in me, I felt cared for. I had two emotionally unavailable parents, I needed someone to show me they cared about me. On this day though, about halfway through lunch, the sexual questions began. I didn't see that coming! Again, my life is turned upside down by the same man! The day proceeds with him buying me a dildo (he felt I needed a "toy" because I was "single"). I refused it and later on he asked to "experiment" with it. He ended things by showing me pornographic magazines; he tried everything to get me interested. He was beyond sick!

Through my research, I realized I was a victim of sexual abuse and he fit the profile of a child molester. He never cared about me, he had been "grooming" me all that time! My family wouldn't face reality. "I read too much," according to them.

"I told you, you hung out with him too much, I tried to warn you." Devastation. My mother was my newest enemy, my biggest betrayer. My head spinning with pure confusion over what I was hearing. Instead of my mother supporting me, like a normal mother would do, I was blamed. I will convince her he is sick, just wait until she hears this.

"He tried to molest me when I was little."

There, my secret was out. Now for sure she will see how sick he is, I'll win her support.

"Why didn't you tell me this happened when you were little?" Again, placing the blame on me. "I am not hearing this!" This is my newest nightmare. I'm blamed, shamed and re-traumatized by my own mother. I was the problem, it was my fault. The message was loud and clear.

Just when I thought the psychological abuse couldn't get any worse, not long after telling my mother, his wife came by my Nonna's house. She pulls me aside into my bedroom, her words made me sick; it apparently, "made her marriage better than ever." That traumatized me on a whole other level.

About three weeks after those sick, twisted conversations with my mom and his wife, my rage gave me the strength to confront this man. I have no idea how I found the courage, but there I was, standing face to face with this sick, twisted man. It was the scariest yet bravest thing I have ever done. I needed answers and I didn't care that I had no support. I needed to stand up for Laura. I couldn't let him get away with this. My mother tried to stop this confrontation, but for once in my life I didn't give a shit about her.

His smirk quickly vanished. After his constant deflections to my questions, I finally let him know, I remembered the "bathtub." Well, he turned bright red and threatened to, "pick me up and throw me out" if I didn't leave! My mother rushed us out not saying one word to him, but to me, yes, pressuring me to put my boots on because I refused to leave.

That day tormented me every single day of my life, not understanding how my mother could just sit there in silence and not stand up for me, her daughter. "I made a promise with his wife not to get involved." I got my answer, 14 years later.

"You keep trying to live your life through someone else," Sandra says. It would take me just over seven years from that first session, to finally start living for myself. My biggest struggle, through it all, was to end this toxic relationship with my mother. I had hope she would change. June 19, 2014 was that day I made the choice to cut her out of my life for good.

I somehow reverted backwards and reached out to her 9 months later, only because some family (ex-family now) convinced me to. As expected, the reply was cold. I could have been dying yet all she cared about was her image. I immediately put her in her place, stood my ground and let her know, she would never again manipulate me. This interaction confirmed for me that she's a severe narcissist who would never change.

My family protected a child molester over protecting me, the victim. I was the "problem" because I stood for the truth. But I was always different from them. I wasn't a girl who lived in denial or false sense of reality. "You lost the love of your family," my mother wrote in an email. Yup, very true. Why? Because I refused to turn a blind eye towards a child molester.

I struggled to break free from a toxic family system, but I did it. It wasn't easy. I was scared shitless so many times at the thought of having no family, but where was my so-called family all those years I needed them? What is family if not the people who are there for you in your darkest moments?

I had to fall so many times before I got it right. I'd take three steps back but five steps forward, gaining strength and courage each step of the way. I was the little engine that could! With the help of Sandra and my Nonno, I gained so much strength. Sandra was my rock and my Nonno was my hero; together they supported, encouraged and believed in me!

The day I broke free was the most empowering day of my life. I finally took my power back! I was just a girl trying to get my family to acknowledge my pain, their damaging behaviour and for us to get help as a family. But that wasn't my job. My job was to take care of Laura.

March 21st, 2016 was the day I received my official legal name change. What a powerful feeling as I create a new identity, a new life, a new legacy for myself. I deserve that. I'm creating the life of my dreams, choosing healthy people that empower and support my life. I choose who I call family. I'm living my truth and living my life on my terms, finally. I feel more empowered than ever and this fierce new me is here to stay!

POOR CHOICES, HUGE LESSONS

Maria Grazia Bevilacqua

Have you ever felt the weight of a huge responsibility in making a crucial decision? That may be against your morals, yet, it's the last straw left to pick?

Let me share a true story, about my dear friend Sabrina, a married woman with a daughter, who lived in Italy. She went from burnout to victory, by finding the courage to forgive herself of her poor choice and take her power back by the lessons she's learned.

I can still hear her trembling voice while telling her story, piercing my heart and touching me to the core, as if I was living it myself, while sipping her tea and gazing out the window: "I remember an evening of May; I was working, driving around the town to collect insurance premiums from my clients. I had decided to take a different route home to avoid going through the town. It was getting really dark. The dirt roads of the country were almost disappearing in the dark. I was stopped at the lights of a small intersection and was staring at a wooden pole with a dim light. I had heard of people getting mugged at this isolated intersection. I was getting anxious and feeling nauseous. I rolled down my window, closed my eyes, breathed in the fresh country air, allowing it to calm my nerves. A sudden jerk of my car startled me. A cold knife under my chin appeared out of nowhere. I stopped breathing. A male voice was whispering in my ear saying he was sent by someone for me to pay my dues!"

Sabrina turned to me with fear in her eyes, clutching her shirt at her chest. "Another hand was caressing my cleavage," she said. "I was horrified! My heart stopped in shock. I couldn't move my head to see who it was. His tone raised, a sudden jerk of his hand pricked my chin with the tip of the blade, just about to puncture my skin. His words were like venom, asking for money back for his friends. I had the vision of my rape and throat slashed. Suddenly, another car was approaching the intersection and the man fled. I slammed my foot on the gas pedal and stopped only when I got home in my driveway." My jaw dropped! As I sat beside her, I held her hand and asked her how she found herself in that situation.

Sabrina's eyes welled up with tears as she started speaking: "You see, years ago, while I was still married, my husband had advanced in his military career and the responsibilities were highly stressful. As a result, he was diagnosed with depression. He was under psychological treatment and I was afraid that he would suddenly quit his job or worse. I was working part-time with a life insurance company for several years and my income wasn't sufficient to support us. I decided to inform his parents of the situation, to seek help, even if my husband didn't want anyone to know. During my conversation, a family member, Joe, happened to be present. After listening, he invited me to follow him away from my in-laws. Joe suggested that the perfect solution was early retirement for my husband and that I should go to work full-time. He mentioned that he had political connections that could get me a government position. All I had to do was pay them for the inconvenience. Joe asked me to not mention anything to anyone, especially my husband, should I decide to pursue his offer, as bribery is illegal, and we could all end up in jail." Sabrina shook her head, looking at me, and continued. "I felt my gut go into knots and was nauseous at the thought of doing something illegal and mostly hiding it from my husband. I thanked Joe for his offer and told him it wasn't for me."

I acknowledged Sabrina for not getting involved. Sabrina turned her face to the window again and then looked at me saying, "I wasn't that smart. I actually later gave in!" She looked down to her cup to hide her shame and took a sip. My eyes opened wider and I gave her an inquisitive look.

"A few months passed by after speaking with Joe," she continued, "and my husband was getting worse. I was so concerned that he could have a moment of weakness and commit suicide. Finding a job was the best solution. Jobs were practically impossible to find because of the recession. That's when I made that decision to buy myself a job!"

I felt the desperation in her voice and understood where she was getting that courage to do such a thing, to save her husband, marriage and happiness.

"I asked Joe, during a family gathering, to let me know what the conditions were for the purchase of a job. He told me that the cost was about $10,000. I didn't personally have that kind of money and asked if I could pay in lump sums as soon as I got the job. Joe's 'connections' would agree to give me my government position if I would find another three people who had the money to 'buy' their jobs. I thought to myself, 'Oh my God! He's crazy to ask me to involve other people in the job deal!'"

Tears started rolling down Sabrina's face as she continued: "I felt so lost and hopeless. The thought of seeing my husband suffer helplessly was devastating me. I cried myself asleep at nights. I found the courage to ask for a loan from my friend who owned a bakery, explaining to her my situation and what I needed it for. She jumped on the opportunity to ask me to get a job for her daughter too. I told her that I didn't want her to get involved. I was doing it out of desperation and asked her to wait first to see if the deal was real with me. She insisted that she wanted to risk it because I was willing to, and promised to be discrete about it. I called Joe and explained to him my friend's intention. I made it clear that I wasn't supporting his deal; it was only because she insisted so badly. I told Joe that I was pulling out of the deal because I didn't have the money and that I would arrange for them to meet… after that… I was out!"

Sabrina took a sip from her cup. "A few weeks went by and I received a phone call from my friend, the baker, inviting me for a coffee at her place. When I got there, another two women who I knew as my insurance clients greeted me with huge smiles and hugs. The three of them were so excited that I had figured out that my friend had told them about the 'job deal.' I wanted to turn around and run out the door! I felt so sick to my stomach. The three of them begged me to see if there was a remote chance to buy another two positions."

Sabrina suddenly straightened up in her chair and leaned forward, looking at me with a twinkle in her eye. "A thrilling thought came to mind. Oh my God! I had a job too! Suddenly that sickness lifted to joy. I decided to just go with the flow and maybe this 'deal' could work after all. The two ladies gave me the documents and their money, which I gave to Joe, who assured me that the four positions were going to be available by the fall or in the New Year, with the retirement of employees in those positions. The four of us were ecstatic!"

Sabrina's tone changed as she continued: "Fall came, the winter passed and spring had arrived. We were starting to get a bit nervous as Joe told us that the positions were still not available and that we needed to be patient for another few months. I had found out that more and more people from my town got involved with Joe. It was getting very ugly! I would receive calls from strangers asking for their money back and was stalked by neighbours."

A wave of fear and anxiety hit me as Sabrina went on: "Another winter came and I was desperate. I had people harass me and threaten to tell my husband. I had lost so much weight, had no appetite and sleepless nights overtook me. This had to end. I found the courage to phone Joe to tell him that my life had become unbearable to live, with harassments and threats of people telling my husband sooner or later. Joe was harsh, threatening to harm my family if I said anything and didn't stick to the plans. He continued saying his 'connections' would be glad to fit me a pair of cement shoes, heavy enough to touch the bottom of the sea, where no one would have found my body, as custom use of the Italian mafia. Joe paused and calmly added that he had the proof of my responsibility of the scheme and that he had nothing to do with it because people gave the money to me. I froze at the sound of the word 'scheme.' Joe involved me in a scheme?! How could have I been so naïve? I had decided to tell my husband at this point, before someone else would. I was on the verge of a nervous breakdown. I started throwing up in my driveway."

Sabrina got up from her chair and went to the window, then came back to the table next to me. She put a hand on my shoulder as she realized I was in tears myself. I asked her how she found the strength and courage to go through it all. She replied, "I left myself in the hands of God and surrendered to my fate. I made the mistake and it was time for me to pay, even if it meant my life." I asked her what had happened next, with her husband knowing. As Sabrina was pouring some more tea in her cup, she sat again at the chair and tears welled up in her eyes, as if she was living it all over again: "I remember, that same night I got assaulted, I had decided to tell my husband. My heart was racing at the thought that he already knew what was happening before I had the chance to tell him. As I was walking through the door, he greeted me with a pale face, closed the doors behind him as he was staring at me. With a firm low voice, he asked, 'what's happening? Who are you?' In that moment I had realized that I didn't even know myself or who I had become. I didn't know where to start. As I tried to open my mouth to speak, the words wouldn't come out. I was shaking, in shock. Tears were welling up, blurring my sight. A whisper peeped out asking for forgiveness, explaining the fact that I didn't realize how bad things were until that moment. The thought of telling my husband about my wanting to 'buy a job' and the worst, involving other people, was getting me sick. I ran to the bathroom to throw up. My husband followed me to the bathroom. I started crying desperately. He picked me up from the floor and shook me, saying, 'you're not capable of this. Who involved you? Tell me the truth.' As I gasped for air, I asked how he found out and that I wished I had told him first. A woman stopped him on his way home and told him that I took her money since last year for some 'job deal,' which never happened and now she wanted her money back. I told him that I had been assaulted that night and that I felt endangered and wanted to run away and hide at my parent's until I came up with a solution." As Sabrina banged her firsts on the table, she continued: "That's when I made the decision to stop everything! I packed up some clothes for us in shopping bags, to not raise suspicion, with the intention of not returning. I had mentioned nothing about Joe, until I felt safe." Sabrina calmly added, "as a punishment of my doing, my husband thought to call a family meeting with his family, forcing me, before going to my parents, to inform them. Joe was there too. I was verbally abused, stripped of my purse, wallet with all my credit cards, cheque book, and money and told that I didn't deserve to be a wife and mother of my child. As those words were piercing my soul, a wave of calmness came through my entire being and I finally knew what I had to do; get a good lawyer and hand myself to the justice. I kept quiet."

Sabrina continued while sipping her tea: "I then went to face my father and told him what was happening. My father lost it! Right away he asked if Joe was involved because of his troubles with the law in the past for the same scheme. I told my dad that I couldn't say anything without speaking to a lawyer first and that I could not go back home, because I would have not survived another week, as I had been threatened. I ended the conversation saying that I felt that the right thing to do was go to the police as soon as possible, even if it meant for me to go to prison. My father was furious, quickly took action and called a family friend criminal lawyer to book an urgent appointment. The lawyer's suggestion was to keep contact with Joe and play his game. I left an affidavit with my lawyer explaining the situation and my intentions to cooperate with the justice in leading the investigations. I informed my husband that I wasn't to have any contact with anyone, for our safety, him included, who agreed to leave me and my daughter at my dad's place. I hid my car and never left the house, nor peeked out of the windows. My lawyer found out that Joe and his 'connections' had been under investigation for over two years and the police were aware of my involvement through phone interceptions. However, authorities couldn't understand to what extent I could have been involved in the planning of the scheme. My affidavit matched exactly what was retrieved from the phone interceptions with Joe. It was clear that I believed every word he said and had no clue of the scheme and was only a victim of the circumstances, just like everyone else. I had wrongly assumed a careless attitude towards the whole situation."

I was so intrigued about her story and was taking mental note of the lessons. No matter how burnt out she was, the courage and wisdom dominated her persona, in making up for her poor choice. Now I was waiting for that link to victory as she continued her story.

"My testimonial had the missing keys to conclude the investigation, to proceed to the arrest of the entire organization. My lawyer suggested for me to leave the country so Joe and his organization would think that I fled, taking all the blame. I had signed an agreement with the authorities to appear in court when called to testify, after leaving the country. In one week I got my passport and plane ticket for Toronto, Canada. I was heart-wretched. My soul was bleeding from the tearing of my emotions of leaving my husband, my friend, our love, my life companion, our dreams and future together."

Sabrina paused as tears rolled down her face. "The day before leaving, I felt the need to meet with my husband to put closure with the situation and that I was cooperating with the justice for the investigations, as it was the least I could do to make things right. I explained to him that arrest warrants were being served soon and it was necessary for me and our daughter to leave the country for our safety, before the arrests. I asked him to not mention anything to his family until we had left and give me full custody of our daughter. He agreed and signed the authorization papers prepared by my lawyer."

At this point I felt a rush of victory over Sabrina's poor choice, as justice prevailed. She was leaving her husband, because of her poor choice, the scheme was getting cleaned up and a new opportunity was prepared for her and her daughter to live a happy and free life.

Sabrina continued: "As I was sitting on the plane, looking out of the window, tears rolled down my cheeks, stinging my face, as my thoughts were with my daughter, who I had to leave behind. Her documents weren't ready, so I told her that my father would bring her to me as soon as possible and that we would have a great life together. I still remember my daughter crying and holding me tight, not wanting me to leave. I cried endlessly to the airport. Those were tears of relief. It was finally over! A sudden comforting thought came to me; a brilliant life was ahead for us, in the land of opportunity. As soon as my daughter reached me, Joe and his 'connections' got arrested and I was called back to Italy to testify and was released from all charges."

A smile of satisfaction and victory filled Sabrina's face, making me understand that it was necessary for her to live that experience to unleash her true power and appreciate her freedom, happiness and successful life raising her daughter on her own.

From Sabrina I have learned to trust that my own gut feeling, God, the Universe, is leading me to happiness. I learned the true meaning of forgiveness of others and especially ourselves, which isn't meant to just release someone from their debt of their offence; it's necessary to move forward in our life journey, to make room for us to grow into our own power, our own victory, after the burnout.

BEING PRESENT

Danielle Joworski

"What is the point of me being here? You don't want me anyway."

"Of course I do," I replied to my daughter as I hurriedly tucked her into bed. "Why would you say that? I love you."

"Because you never seem to want me around and I always seem to be in the way," my daughter spat out at me, her young voice vibrating with emotion.

I immediately stopped organizing the stuffed animals on her bed and stood there, stiff and collecting my thoughts that were racing in my head as I fought back the tears that welled up in my eyes. I felt a pit open in my stomach that was hollow and empty, just like the emotions my daughter expressed when she shared her thoughts. I moved closer to her so that she could see me better in the dark room, with just the light from the hallway providing the only source of illumination. I could see tears glistening in her eyes and her whole face had a soft look to it, but it had sadness that was obvious.

I had to take a deep breath in order to gain control of my emotions before I said a word. It wasn't enough. I needed to take a second breath.

"Honey, if there is something that I do know, it is that I do love you. I'm sorry that you feel the way that you do. What do you want from me?" I asked her gently using a soft voice and trying to project as much love into it as I could. I knew she wanted time together, and that as a parent I should be offering it unconditionally, but I wanted to get more insight into how she was feeling and seeing herself in the family dynamic.

"I'd like to do things together, just you and I. If I'm good all week will you do something with me this weekend?" she asked timidly, not able to look me in the eyes.

I gently turned her head towards me so that she could look into my eyes and feel like I was connecting with her.

"Just focus on being who you are and we will spend mommy-daughter time together this weekend. I promise."

My daughter seemed to be happy with my response as she provided me with a meek smile as I kissed her forehead, wiped her bangs out of her eyes and smiled back at her before leaving the room and heading straight into mine to shed my own tears.

Those words stung me to the core and haunted me for months. I knew at the time that I had been increasingly emotionally absent as I struggled to be able to 'do it all' while making it all look so easy. "Doing it all" meant having a career with progressive growth, being the primary caregiver who stayed home when the kids were sick, and providing my kids with the opportunities that I did not have as a child. In most cases, I was physically present, but emotionally and mentally absent. My thoughts in any moment were focused on the multitude of other activities that I needed to complete, or looking at my phone to see who needed me on the other end of an email or text, oblivious to the fact that my kids, who were right in front of me, needed me more.

My daughter's words scared me. How as a parent could I be providing love and emotional absence at the same time? It was an oxymoron of feelings. That night once I finally fell into bed, I could not sleep. All that was racing through my mind were my daughter's words and as I heard the words, the emotions I felt at that exact moment rushed back. I cried myself to sleep that night.

I was failing as a mother. One of my biggest fears had come to fruition.

During the many sleepless nights that followed, I did a lot of reflecting on my life, my role in it and how I was contributing to it. I could no longer avoid what was becoming obvious; my life priorities were out of whack. Not only was my daughter feeling like she was not an integral part of the family, through my actions I was not even an integral part of my family. Time was spent focused on work. I had literally turned into a boarder in my own home. I was no longer a wife but a roommate; somebody to split the bills with.

I was burnt out from trying to 'do it all.' I had a vision of who I was meant to be and I disappointed myself regularly because I felt that I was not serving others to my greatest potential. This tear-inducing scenario with my daughter was one of many examples of how I felt, like I was disappointing others and myself.

I was failing as a wife, a career woman, a mom and most of all, I was failing myself.

I was tired of working hard just to feel like a failure but it was like I was shackled in my ability to think or make decisions. I felt like I was standing in a field with my arms stretched out, my body like a star with the points representing all the different elements of my life. The points were all turned inward, causing me pain. Anything I did at the time, such as re-prioritizing or spending more time with my family, was short lived and did nothing to reduce the pain I felt.

A lone walk I took one day to clear my head provided me with a reprieve from my pain, but it brought new feelings of terror. The reprieve was from a thought that intuitively I knew was correct, but it was radical and I had always been a pretty logical person. It was a thought that in order to change my results, I needed to change how I was living my life. The thought was that I needed to leave my job.

The problem was I feared making changes, even though I did not like the current results in any element of my life. It was familiar, what I knew and was sadistically comfortable with. Once I opened the floodgate of thoughts that revolved around the growing belief that I needed to make a drastic change, I struggled to gain a sense of balance in my life.

I was grossly aware that in order to regain balance, repair the rifts I had created in my family and search for a sense of who I was, I needed time; time I did not have in the unbalanced lifestyle I had created through the decisions I had been making, yet time needed to breathe life back into me. So I created voluminous amounts of time. I had an emotional discussion with my husband. I leveraged emotions from the walk I had taken a few days earlier. I made the decision to commit to myself and my family, to take control and be accountable for my behaviours and actions, and I resigned from my career.

I knew to get out of the state I was in that it would have to take something pretty dramatic and transformational. Resigning definitely fit those categories. Once I resigned, I had time to reflect and see that one of the reasons why I lacked self-confidence was because I had belittled myself down to ticking off as many boxes as I could to feel like I was accomplishing something. That made me realize that I had to move into a mindset of being empowered to control my day-to-day activities so that boxes were not just ticked off, they were permanently removed.

My long road to victory over my dark days spent crying in the shower, with the noise of the water deafening my cries so that nobody would know I was falling to pieces, was marked by a change in mindset. I began to feel empowered and confident in the self-belief that I would put the puzzle of my life back together, exactly how I wanted it. I was done watching my life pass me by, viewing it and not participating in it. I had become a participant who would exercise control, make decisions and steer my life onto a path that would lead to happiness.

Did I know what happiness even was? Sadly, the answer was no.

Without a description of what happiness was, I knew I needed to seek out others who could help me define it. I realized that after so many years of not devoting my time to activities and a lifestyle that focused on me I had lost all sense of who I was. I needed to find a process that would reconnect me with who *I really* was. I owed my family that. I owed myself that.

I knew that in order to re-build years of habits and behaviors, I needed to make changes that would reconstruct who I was so that I would not revert back to the unsatisfactory behaviours I was working on ridding. Resigning was the first drastic change I needed. I then needed to devote time to a process whereby I could be taught how to take control over my decisions and my life, and re-build myself. Nobody else could do that but me; I knew I needed help though. A checklist with tick boxes would not work to sustain a transformational change in myself.

I did not have to look long or far for somebody who could help me. The universe works in such wondrous ways. An angel had appeared to me months prior in the form of a mentor who had guided me as I focused energy on changing my professional life. Never could I have foretold that it would be my personal life that would be in an upheaval; a personal life that required overcoming fears of intimacy in order to create room for personal growth. I needed to open to intimacy through a high degree of vulnerability to openly share and dissect repressed feelings and emotions that were holding me back from being who I truly was.

I was not a touchy-feely person and sharing my feelings made me uncomfortable. I had grown comfortable in being an emotionally closed-off person. It was how I had protected myself, and now my angel was gently supporting me as I peeled off my layers of armour. Like nails running down a chalk board I would grit my teeth and wince as I talked about myself and became aware of why I behaved the way I did. Quickly though, discomfort was replaced with serenity as I began to forgive my past behaviours and myself. An emotional journey I needed to take.

For me, having a mentor felt like therapy, with me divulging my inner thoughts but with one big difference; mentoring included an emotional connection that I needed in order to change. My angel listened to my woes and challenges, never judging, but providing me with the tools to dig into the layers of my subconscious to fully understand who I was and how I could change. I refer to my mentor as an angel because the wings of support and unconditional love were wrapped around me as guidance was provided. Those facets became the stepping stones I trepidatiously tiptoed on after I resigned. I was not sure-footed during my journey working on getting brutally honest with myself and changing my negative habits and paradigms, yet I continued on.

By breaking down the sub-conscious paradigms I had built, pieces of my true self started to shine through, like a bright light, full of energy and focused. To further ignite myself out from a burnt out life, I needed to formulate a purpose or goal out of a question that I consistently asked myself: *what do I want?* It needed to be something I would feel passionate about and serve as my foundation when I got scared and wanted to retreat back to old behaviors. I needed something I would be accountable for and that would provide focus to my streaming light so that I could feel it burning inside me, providing the fuel for me to continue to make strides forward.

I realized that without a goal I was just a physical presence, being in a body and moving throughout a life I felt disconnected to. Defining a goal shifted my perception from being in a life to having life. From sitting in the front row of a movie theatre with popcorn and beverage in hand watching a movie about my life to being the producer, director and star. I could make myself the heroine and not the victim. It meant taking responsibility and accountability for my results, which were based on my actions and behaviours and nobody else's.

Having a goal helped to remove and eliminate the noises and negative self-talk that had been interrupting my thoughts and adding to the social identity crisis I had been having. At the time I resigned I could not clearly define who I was or what I wanted to be. Mom? Career-women? A blend of both? I created purpose within my life as my goal focused on me succeeding instead of failing, of me becoming an author and helping to empower women and girls.

Once I had my goal, I had to make it clear so that I could visualize the end result. The ability to see the end result was crucial for keeping me emotionally connected and moving forward. I visualized sales numbers, book promotions and, most importantly, being the mom I wanted to be.

I wrote out the negative self-talk that I told myself and defined its opposite, positive version; overwhelmed was replaced with empowered, lack of balance turned into controlled decisions, disconnection with self blossomed into loving myself, fearful was beaten down by brave, alone vanished with the presence of abundant friendships, and self-limiting was erased with limitless potential. These lists turned into positive affirmations that I repeated daily to help build my confidence.

> *I am empowered.*
> *I am able to make controlled decisions.*
> *I am able to love myself unconditionally.*
> *I am brave.*
> *I am blessed with abundant relationships.*
> *I am gifted with limitless potential.*

Having a mentor, a goal that I was passionate about and saying positive affirmations were the key components in my victorious journey. They provided the direction I needed when I felt I was in the dark and maneuvering through life without a map. My goal also served as the focal point of conversations and alliances that I established with others, and because the goal included a timeline, it helped to keep me accountable for my actions.

As I began to move confidently towards my goal, my life began to change. The lives of my family began to change. Harmony began to filter into the household, replacing what was once discontent. I was aware that my past behaviors were the root cause to the previous disharmony. I knew that I had not gotten enough sleep, did not have a healthy diet and that the blending of these two behaviors caused me to have a negative attitude. I knew that I was prioritizing work over family with money and career defining my success, and not seeing my beautiful family as a success.

I have now accepted and embraced myself for the woman, wife and mother that I am. I can't go back and change what was, just use it to remind me of how much my family and I have evolved. I am now empowered to take control of my life, to continually connect with and be passionate about personal goals and use my experience of being completely burnt out to remind me that I was able to wage a war against myself and come out victorious.

My victory did not happen overnight. It took months of writing my goals out and reflecting on positive affirmations daily. I started to enjoy talking about my fears with others as it became cathartic, as it was soothing to learn that I was not alone in my perception that as a mom, I felt pressure to do and be everything for everybody. Although I was victorious from battling how I used to see myself, it was really from being vulnerable and sharing what I thought were my limiting characteristics.

My victory was being able to recognize and love the reflection that looked back at me in the mirror. A reflection that once was tired and too thin is now confident with a vibrant glean in my eyes and a positive outlook on life. Victory was finding the balance that was needed in my life in order to appreciate it and be ever present in it, no longer just participating in it.

My daughter and I now have a set of questions we ask each other at night as I tuck her into bed that are positive and supportive.

"Mom, what was your favourite thing about today?" She asks happily, initiating the conversation.

I reply from my position on the side of her bed in her brightly lit room, no longer dark.

"And what was your challenge today?" she inquires with interest as she likes that I share with her the learning moments I find within my challenges.

"And what are you looking forward to tomorrow?" She enjoys hearing about what adventures I might have planned for the next day.

My victory is about more than me and the life I created for myself. It is also about learning how to prioritize time with my daughter and my family, providing them with the love and physical presence that they need and deserve.

.

LOVE UNFOLDING

Jenny McKaig

It's early morning. I gaze at the growing mound beneath my two growing mounds of breast, a belly that's expanding as I am. I see a roundness I never knew before, save one whirlwind trip to Europe where I had planned to be there eight weeks and ended up staying six months.

I was blessed with the most generous, caring hosts in cities smattered throughout Western Europe—a collection of my uncle's friends and friends of a sweet, Italian immigrant family from my hometown in Canada—an eclectic couple with a lanky, young son in Strasbourg, France; a sweet, trendy family in Grosseto, Italy; a quirky savoir-faire lawyer who had a spare apartment in Munich, Germany; and a hearty, welcoming family who insisted I "eat, eat" in Rome, Italy.

I think that family in Rome loved gelato; the heart of their love and giving in food, great nurturing, comfort food of pizza and pasta—so much pasta!—the grandest lunches, savoury with sweet finishes, and modest dinners, so heart-warming when everyone gathered around to eat. Each family member toured me throughout the Romanesque architecture, ancient buildings and majestic monuments, and ending with the sweetest delight: "I know the best gelato place in all of Rome."

My Roman touring followed escapades along the Tuscan seaside and, previous to that, a rustic home nearby the heart of European Parliament, Strasbourg, where I learned about sumptuous cheese, partnered with bread and wine. "Zee stinkier zee cheese, zee better," the mom-host said to me, sharing brie and camembert and cheeses I was too young to note the name of but old enough to know they melted in my mouth like pure magic.

That food, in Europe, tasted like what I imagine heaven to be.

The thing is, we get to receive heaven, in tender moments and presence in all our experiences of life—if we let ourselves.

Gazing down now at my growing mounds of belly and breasts, I feel a moment of peace. My ever-rounding body is usually fit or thin, with the exception of that indulgent jaunt in Europe when I got home and had to wear skirts all summer because I couldn't fit in any of my pants. This miracle inside me though is changing my body, a blessing.

I'm experiencing the newness, growing a baby and being months from becoming a parent, because I let myself live the fullness of all the moments of my journey. That means travels in Europe, Australia, Asia and the Americas, yes, but it also means moments of grace, everyday adventures and going for life with a grit to live it with all I've got. I didn't foresee having a husband, for example, or at least wavered between wanting one (and in my heart, truly wanting that deep, fulfilling relationship) and not letting myself love myself enough to be wholly loved. That is, of course, until a series of weeks or days or possibly even years where I ignited the flame of truth, that unrelenting belief and deep knowledge within that I am worth it, I can have it all.

I can live an even greater life than any I had ever envisioned or even the one that unfolded for me daily, which upon looking back was already pretty blessed and definitely very full.

Around the time I made a conscious choice to start nudging myself towards deepening or discovering some kind of internal love—that determination of 'loving myself' a ubiquitous and often fleeting phrase, yet one I was resolute in securing for myself—I began to connect with a love deeper and more real than skin and greater than what I learned to be soul, radiating from the inside out.

I began to love me for me, wholly, fully, beautifully, battle scars and all, inside and out.

For years, I had a battle in relationship with my body. I was grateful for the recovered function of legs that once didn't work after a basketball accident left me unable to walk, still I was socialized in the way young women are to hate the external. I loathed the sight of a hint of excess fat, or any perceptive imperfection. It was this loathing of my body, thin, fit, it didn't matter in my young eyes—the bottom line, it felt never good enough. I visualized cutting off the insides of my thighs, grabbing what was barely fat and pinching it, seeing a blade in my mind to slice those unwanted extras society told me I shouldn't have.

In later teen years and into my early twenties, I took laxatives; copious handful amounts of "all-natural" laxatives, as though the natural label made it okay to swallow so many at once, despite the pains and cramping in my stomach and violent diarrhea to follow. I did this, somehow simultaneously, while living radiantly, joyfully, grasping every ounce of life to live it fully.

The dichotomy is as complex as humans ourselves. What I know is this though, I didn't love myself fully—not as a whole.

The time came years later, amidst whirlwind travels, listening to life's callings and dancing the cha-cha of one step forward, two steps back, those moments of life that felt like I had lived a thousand lifetimes in this one here on earth—I made the choice. I would learn to love myself, discover myself whole, be whole, and live the love that I am.

Ironically all this came through a body image seminar and what felt like years of seeking the deeper purpose of who I am. I left that seminar changed. I wrote a blog titled, 'Fear and Self-Loathing in Fitness,' me being a fitness and wellness instructor at the time, but it wasn't just fear and self-loathing in fitness, it was rampant in all of society. Every phrase degrading, every billboard loudly claiming, you are not good enough.

I began to know a new truth though; I was good enough. I am good enough, whole and complete, as perfect as the illusion of perfection can be, with all my imperfections. In moments of awkward 'learning to love myself,' I began with my body, standing naked in front of a mirror and seeing myself, really seeing myself, taking sage advice to see the meat-suit that carries my soul with curiosity and fascination instead of hatred and distaste. At the same time, I set fire to my soul. I was meditating regularly and often reaching what's called a state of Samadhi, euphoria or bliss, a transcendent state.

It's funny that in later years this energetic transcendence actually changed my physical appearance, making me look younger, more vibrant than my thirty-something years might claim. When I eventually learned to awaken the cells of my body, each strand of DNA having a telomere that activates on the cellular level, I found myself rejuvenated, refreshed, feeling energized and with people commenting on how alive I am—the energy, they say—and how young I look, too.

It's in letting go that I've been able to renew.

It wasn't always this way though. I remember a time where, on the surface, people may have commented on my vibrancy, too. A fit, perceptively healthy, exuberant young fitness and wellness instructor, I did have a way to dig in and help motivate others. The challenge was, I was giving from an empty cup. I was emotionally barren, or at least scraped so dry I just didn't have a true vibrancy from which to give. I hadn't yet connected with that deeper sense of self, a knowing, and the heart of who I really am, so in part my time then was a rat-race of superficial energy glutton. I was like a kid who ate five packs of Smarties, wild and thrashing, hyper and carefree, but when those Smarties wore off—woah. I was teaching 20, and sometimes 25 or more fitness classes in a week, each an hour long and often doing two or three hours of weightlifting classes in one day. At the rate of pay of a fitness and wellness instructor in Toronto, those 25-plus classes barely scraped the bucket of bills, so I topped the exercise schedule with freelance writing and editing gigs and bartending—and I was in school full-time.

My body hurt. My mind hurt. I was physically, emotionally, intellectually and spiritually exhausted. In teaching, I was meant to be the pillar of health, a role model cueing fitness from the front of the room; like so many of those in fitness, I didn't, at that time at least, walk my talk. I summoned energy for a class, music driving me, the want to please and have a class love me surging through me to be the best instructor I could be; then when I got home, I would chug a liter of orange juice because my blood sugar was so off, and collapse on the couch, dredging myself up only to finish writing gigs or schoolwork or race to get ready for a bartending shift.

It was then that, though I could muster a face of bravado, smiles and encouragement, even tips that were true—healthy lifestyle knowledge not equating to walking the talk—I hadn't yet connected with that deeper sense of self.

The changes began. Although fitness, an industry meant to support health, was hurting my body and reaping havoc in my life, it was also opening me to those seeds of knowledge that would change me. I began by teaching an intensive aerobics class, something literally called BodyATTACK, and though I chide the name, it was a lot of fun. As with anything, there are limits. Intense, elite-athlete type cardio and excessive strenuous weightlifting can take its toll. I began teaching lighter classes, training in yoga, tai chi and Pilates, classes more caring for the body, and eventually did my mind-body accreditation.

In my exploration of meditation, I began to see a calm, a peace, and I knew the pace I was living at had to change. I took a four-month whirlwind stint, putting a pause on everything accelerated, and moved to the sleepy foothills of Tucson, Arizona, where all I did was enjoy life, do yoga and write. Shortly after I was back, I got a corporate wellness job that was amazing—until it wasn't. I no longer had to teach an insane amount of classes, nor did I race from multiple jobs and school, chaos jumbled, and I had a great salary and even benefits, a dream for many in the wellness world. I was also still writing on the side, and deepening my practice of yoga and meditation.

Even with a great job, the changes were stirring in me, surfacing to the brim. In continued meditation, a commitment to journaling and the spark of a knowing that there could be more for me in this life, I found myself on the pristine beaches of Tulum, Mexico, at a dance retreat. It was more a time to connect than anything else; soul sisters I'd meet, precious and beautiful and radiant, experiencing similar questions as I was—burnout? Sometimes, yes. A harkening desire to dance with life in a new way, one that nurtured and supported, instead of pushed and prodded, and that deepest desire to live more purposefully, to know and experience greater meaning—it was what we were all after.

Even if only for the moments on the beach. My toes swirling in the sand, water rippling, an iPod on and moving my body in a way that allowed me to connect not just with physical activity—it was barely about the physical activity—but with a precious creativity, my body an instrument, music and energy seeping from fingertips to toes, connecting earth, sea and the beautiful souls who danced the beach together.

I had moments of despair there, too. There was an emptying. We spoke daily on topics that meant something; presence, communication, sense of self. Living for ourselves, rebelliously sometimes, unapologetically always, because we're the only ones we live with for all our life.

I presented my first ever writing workshop on those white sands of Mexico. Meditating on the beach, connecting in a Samadhi state, the euphoria of connection and creativity radiating within; I received a lightbulb moment. Words were moving through me so quickly—I opened my eyes and grabbed my pen, I could barely get them down in time.

When I looked at the page, I saw an outline for what would become my signature workshop, *Unleash the Writer Within*. With soul sisters and friends on the beach, many of whom I had known two or three days, I led those ladies. In fingertips to pen, and pen to page, words and sometimes tears and snorts and sniffles and laughs flowing as they breathed and began that utmost powerful feat: expressing. Clinking glasses of red wine to begin, a now dear soul friend having brought a bottle of merlot to toast the occasion, I said, "you must know you do *not* have to drink to write." I enjoyed a sweet sip of wine with a chuckle—in earlier years, I thought I had to be somber, depressive, isolated, the ever-elusive and angst-ridden writer who was cynical or hurting or just plain miserable to be around.

This was hard for me, because it wasn't my nature. The emptying though. There were times over a few years where I had deep, deep release. It was as though I was an excavator of sorrow. Deep in my tissues, the cells of my body clearing, my mind clearing, perhaps even clearing the speckles of dirt and dust that had settled on my soul.

I know now that dark moments do not have to be the way. Just like we don't need to drink to write, desperate and desolate images of writers and starving artists embedded in our society's memory; we also don't need to be sorrowful to know ourselves for who we really are.

It's ironic because I had to move through that, in order to know it. In the movement on the beach, the meditation, choosing joyful activities like dance and creativity, listening to the call of writing and letting myself whittle words, cursive or typed or scribbled on sandwich napkins… I found joy. I chose joy, because it is, quite simply, a better way to live.

It did mean difficult choices so I could honour myself with joy and self-love. Self-love doesn't equate to anger or resentment or feeling stuck and stifled. Self-love is the gentle nudge that says, *you can do it. You're worth it. Keep going in the direction of your dreams.*

Thus the changes. A love affair with myself, going on creative dates and singing in the shower—"you are so beautiful, to me…" and "this little light of mine, I'm going to let it shi-ine…" filled my mornings and raised my frequency, voice and vibration lifting me through what could have felt like challenging times. I left the then-partner who didn't see my seeking and growth as a good thing. I left the amazing, then not-so-amazing, corporate job. I chose joy, love, connectedness, me.

I think that's why I can see my body alive with a renewed appreciation now. Something had shifted. My cells know a new reality, awakened to the truth of lightness within me. When I later began seeing my husband-to-be, I told him he needed to tell me every day that I'm beautiful. It may sound strange, but it's something that helped me. I was reminding myself, and I created the environment and surrounded myself with loving people who could remind me, too. "You're beautiful," he would say, then leave me love notes that read, "Dear Beautiful," or something else equally sweet that made me smile. It was only possible because I had made the leap and chosen to love myself, too.

Loving myself meant later giving birth to a business, now two businesses, and excelling through even the most challenging of moments. The energetic connection I had with myself, that deep self-love and greater knowing that I am a strong woman living my path of purpose, naturally emblazoned my business. Opportunities opened like never before. At first, and like anything new in life, I was an awkward, learning, growing writer who really didn't know much about being a businessperson. I knew in my heart I wanted to continue writing, and with every connection in meditation or going inward, I received strong guidance of the new ways I could be of service and help more people.

I soon discovered that the techniques I had learned both to write fluidly and easily, and to honour the process and awaken a joyful, creative way of being, would transform the lives of many. The number of people who tell me they want to write, or create something, or live a more joyful, purposeful life, caught in the grist and feeling dumped on by the tasks of the everyday, is astounding. In my self-love, I was given gifts of elevating beyond this, and they are not just for me, but also to positively affect the lives of others. Sharing these gifts, and facilitating space so more people can create, love themselves wholly, live joyfully and write, too, is an integral aspect of my core business, and one I am so glad for as it nurtures my soul.

Unleash the Writer Within, my signature course, grew from that outline on the beach in Mexico to a full-day course hosted in cities across Ontario, Canada, and online to attendees around the world. Women and men are becoming authors in my course, *Become a Published Author*, and in working privately with me, and I am beyond blessed to get to guide them on their journey. From those initial days of baby-stepping my way into business, I have not only learned the ropes, I've also grown with an incredible full-time staff and partnered with some pretty phenomenal organizations internationally. Promoters and event organizers host me in speaking, allowing me to share the purpose and passion I live in my business, the unique writing techniques I teach, and how to live a more creative, joyful and passionate life. I have also become a certified digital marketer, so my course, *Become a Copywriting Rockstar*, helps those with purposeful businesses not only write more magnetic copy, but also reach more of the people who need their help.

And now, my sweet.

My team of support is not just professional; family and friends, and my husband-to-be are pillars within my life—all because I decided to first love me. My husband-to-be, the one I couldn't help but open my heart to, is a consistent calling to be the best version of me. A soulmate isn't one who stands by, cheering you on no matter what. That person ignites within you the fire for you to be the most evolved version of yourself. They invite you to balance your life, showing all the areas where cracks can let light in, and they call on you to expand, ever-growing in the lightness of who you are called to be.

A soulmate awakens the aspects of you that are dormant, or in hibernation, waiting and wanting and longing to be discovered. When you meet that person, they can't help but see you for who are you, deeply into your soul, even if they wouldn't describe it that way—which I'm sure my husband-to-be wouldn't.

A man who does this is an exceptional specimen, though they are growing as I see more men in that nurturing, supportive and soulfully awake state; even in their groundedness and keeping it super real.

A woman who does this for herself is allowing all of this to become possible; that crucial evolution of the planet. She says to herself, and the world, *I deserve love. I can live my purpose. I can, in fact, have it all.*

I gaze again at my ever-rounding body, the vehicle that supports my journey. I know there's a sweetness of love inside me; my "LP," our little person as we call her, the baby we will meet later this year. It's love. A blessing. I'm looking outward now, sun rising on the stunning Rocky Mountains of Western Canada. Our pup, Bailey, sleeps nearby. My husband-to-be begins to stir. The day is new. My journey, blessed by love and the deepening of a willingness to go within; continued choices I make, and am so glad I do as they fill my life every day.

continued choices I make, and am so glad I do as they fill my life every day.

CONCLUSION

It's winter, in the Rocky Mountains in Canada. We're wrapping up editing with this book, and I am so moved by each of these authors. I'm journeying with my husband-to-be, on route to enjoy time with family in Whistler, British Columbia, and the scenery is gorgeous. It's amazing, when we step into our power and own who we really are—empowered women and, yes, empowered men, too—we can begin to really thrive in our lives in ways we might have once thought unimaginable.

As I take a moment to breathe in the scenery breezing by, rocky cliffs matched by the splendor of snow-capped mountains and openness of lakes that seem to appear out of nowhere, I think about the authors of this book.

Every single one of them has touched my heart in the most rare, warming and sincere of ways. Each author is so unique, yet their commonalities are strong, the synchronicities of life prominent in each of their stories, and even in the way they are, as people.

As a writer, editor and awakening coach who focuses on helping people get their message to the masses, it is such an honour to work with truly special individuals who are willing to open themselves, be vulnerable, and go for it in writing.

It is no easy feat to understand our lives, let alone dive in to write those experiences and then share them with the world. It's a bravery, a courage and, as Brene Brown, an expert on human connection says, "most people believe vulnerability is weakness. But really, vulnerability is courage. We must ask ourselves… Are we willing to show up and be seen?"

It's that willingness to show up and be seen; those pure, unadulterated, unapologetic, real and raw selves that each of these authors have bared in sharing their stories with you, the reader. I hope and trust that their courage encourages you to show up and be seen in your life, to be exactly who you are, without fear and with a tremendous amount of self-love.

I see in myself commonalities with each of the authors, a connection that threads throughout our entire consciousness and, not only on the etheric level, but on the very real and raw level of human experience, too. I know how transformative writing stories can be, and I know they can also deeply affect those who read them. If you see yourself in any of these stories, smile, and know you are not alone. You are supported. We're all in this together.

~~~

On the way to Whistler, some of the roads are, quite frankly, insane. There's nothing but a small guard rail between cars flying along at speeds unheard of for these winding roads, where it's much technical driving. The speed limit is 120 kilometers per hour. That's 72 miles an hour.

In life, sometimes there's not much between us and falling deep down a cliff. I think of Calli, her courageous journey to not only change her life for the better, and become the person she's called to be, but also the very physical journey of driving these very roads, solo. Uhaul in tow, her sweet Mylo that helped her make the positive changes, and a gut-wrenching knowledge that she could do better; she could have better, and she would.

It's the same empowerment I see and know of Natalie's story. Her choice to take her power back and give herself knowledge so she could make informed decisions and not let the battle with her mind take over. Giving herself tools and a support system to really succeed.

This is what it's about.

These are the threads, along with so many more in the pages of this book, that show us the depth of human experience and—in the courage of each of these brave authors—the fortitude that's available, at any given time, to keep going, to persevere.

I travel with my husband-to-be right now, and I'll be meeting with my father, step-mom, siblings and step-siblings. It's the men I'm thinking of. I've been blessed with an incredibly supportive father, brother, husband-to-be, and a number of men who really get it. They know what it means to be a great human, inside and out. Sabbir's story of perseverance shows not only his own determination and grit, but also the softer side, a tenderness and a strength of being empowered by, and providing deep empowerment of, women.

We are all of course human. There has been a pendulum swing though for many years and, unfortunately, there is still a deep undercurrent of misogynistic trends that needs to be eliminated from our society. Banding together in strength, across all sexes, is the way to create a unified and equal experience, and to better our world for generations to come.

It's not all a great fight, or a battle, either. Women are beautifully connected, nurturing, collaborative, strong, and deeply connected in a way that the feminine energy of this planet has been calling for. A balancing. As Lisa Bartello so beautifully says in her chapter, the Yin and the Yang.

~ ~ ~

We arrive at this picturesque resort in Whistler, British Columbia. I'm about to enjoy some time with family, a balance from the work I've been putting in. I think of Ellie. Randi. Heather. Self-care and time for ourselves. Persevering against the odds and going for it—whether opening ourselves to slowing down, or going for it in the moments that matter.

There's a beautiful, radiant glow from the trees on the mountains. Although it's a journey to visit, it feels like a journey home, like Marla, back to the heart of who each of us are.

Words cannot adequately describe the beauty of each author in the book. They have bared their hearts to you, the intimate details of their lives and innermost thoughts, dreams, feelings and aspirations. They have shown us the truth that's available for all us: we choose in any given moment, and we can live the lives we dream of, no matter what life brings our way.

I hope you have enjoyed this book. I hope it's brought you exactly what you need, when you need it—and I invite you to share it with those you think will enjoy it, too.

The authors of this book are the girlfriends you can call on for support, to bring more harmony to you in all you do.

Please visit the Bios & Resources section and connect with those who have inspired you, informed you, or even just those whose stories you absolutely adore.

Here's to the empowerment of *all* of us—to leading the lives we're here to live, and being empowered along the journey!

RESOURCES & BIOS

Calli Jensen

Calli Jensen is a self-made successful entrepreneur who dedicates her time to empowering women to look and feel great. Calli has a passion for fashion and is committed to improving the lives and self-image of women all around the world. She spends most of her time working her business on social media and connecting with people. She is committed to leaving a lasting impact on everyone she comes in contact with. In her spare time, Calli enjoys fitness, traveling and shopping. Her motivation to get out of bed every morning stems from working towards retiring and being able to travel the world with her mother, Judi. Calli's greatest joy is hearing from her clients how amazing they feel, and how much her products have truly changed their body image and overall health.

Email - Calli@sweetndeadlyfashion.com
Instagram - @sweetndeadlywaisttrainers & @callij_Sweetndeadly
Facebook - biz page https://www.facebook.com/sweetndeadly.gear/
Facebook group - https://www.facebook.com/groups/waisttrainers/
Linkedin - https://www.linkedin.com/in/calli-jensen-247b8961

Danielle Joworski

Danielle Joworski made a radical decision to change careers and follow her life passion of writing to educate and lead others to increase their personal wellness. As an International Bestselling Author, Freelance Writer and Author Coach, she incorporates her background in leadership, corporate writing and adult education to help others share the stories of themselves or their life passion – their companies. Many of her published works are written to inspire women to harness their own innate abilities and apply them positively in their daily lives. In her first book, *The ATHENA Prodigies: Empowering Women Empowering Girls*, Danielle pulled from her own life lessons to motivate and empower women to connect with their intuition and mentor young girls to pursue their own dreams. Active in her community, Danielle volunteers for organizations that provide education, resources and mental health support to girls and teens and is involved in supporting and promoting shared communities for women.

Email - danielle@athenaprodigies.com
Website - http://www.daniellejoworski.com
Facebook - https://www.facebook.com/athenaprodigies/
Twitter - https://twitter.com/athenaprodigies

Ellie Savoy

Ellie Savoy is author of the #1 international bestselling book, **Stop Dieting Start Living: 5 Foundations for Your Health to Permanently Lose Weight Without Dieting Starvation or Suffering in Silence,** and is a Board Certified Holistic Health Coach. When Ellie was diagnosed with uterine fibroids, she later found that it was a "gift in disguise," which led her to a journey of self-healing, and she ended up stumbling upon the real secret to weight loss. Her mission is to help yo-yo dieters get off the dieting merry-go-round permanently, and discover the simplicity and joy of investing in their most precious asset—a healthy mind, body and soul.

Ellie also helps others to show up in their own life, stop making excuses, shift their mindset, have a plan and connect with the passion in their bellies to live their best life. It's a lot of fun!

Ellie lives in the scenic Hudson Valley, New York where she enjoys supporting local farmers, being active in her community and chatting with anyone who wants to ask her a question about how they can get on a healthier and happier path.

To meet Ellie and get a free copy of her book, *Stop Dieting Start Living,* visit: http://elliesavoy.com/free-book

Phone - 845 677 9403
Facebook - https://www.facebook.com/DietFreeAndHealthy
Twitter - https://twitter.com/dietfreehealth
YouTube - https://www.youtube.com/user/dietfreeandhealthy
Instagram - https://www.instagram.com/dietfreeandhealthy/

Heather Gordon

Heather is a savvy business owner who has made a positive impact on her small community. She believes in passion and perseverance, which is brought to light in her chapter. Heather has a bachelor's degree in Logistic Management and Marketing from Central Michigan University and is licensed in cosmetology. She uses her education and passion to influence young women entrepreneurs and supports employees who want to further their education and become successful in all aspects of life. She believes in filling that void: dreaming big and being big. Heather sits on numerous boards, including the Chamber of Commerce, Downtown Development Advisory, and the Arc. She is dedicated to empowering women and pushing them to be the best they can be!

Twitter - http://twitter.com/thehgsalon
Website - http://www.thehgsalon.com
Facebook - https://www.facebook.com/HG-Salon
Instragram - thehgsalon
Pinterest - hgsalon

Jennifer Douglas

Jennifer Douglas is wife to an amazing husband, Rob, and mom to two beautiful children, Summer and Kieran. Jennifer spent most of the early years of her life in a swimming pool, and represented Canada on the National Swim Team. She attended UCLA on a swimming scholarship, where she majored in communication studies and earned the role of swimming team captain. Since graduating from UCLA, Jennifer has spent over ten years in sales and business development, and has found her passion in working as a realtor and writing. When she's not busy helping clients with their real estate needs, Jennifer enjoys blogging about her adventures with two children under the age of three, and spending time outdoors with her family.

Website - www.jenniferdouglas.ca
Facebook - https://m.facebook.com/JenniferDouglasRealEstate/

Jenny McKaig

Jenny McKaig, CEO, Writer & Coach at JennyMcKaig. com, Senior Editor and Co-author, *Empowering Women to Succeed*, Volumes 1 and 2, BAH Professional Writing, accredited Mind-Body specialist and certified Awakening Coach, is an award-winning writer and visionary entrepreneur who empowers with transformational stories to raise global consciousness and elevate success. Jenny's signature course, *Unleash the Writer Within*, and her copywriting and book-writing courses, *Become a Copywriting Rockstar and Become a Published Author* have changed the lives and businesses of participants around the world. Jenny's proficiency with language is matched only by her love of surfing, yoga, travel adventures, her husband Shawn, their pup Bailey and daughter-on-the-way, LP—not in that order.

Website - http://www.jennymckaig.com/
Facebook - https://www.facebook.com/jmwrites
Twitter - https://twitter.com/JennyMcKaig

Laura Vella

Laura is currently pursuing her childhood dream; to be an actor. She's passionate about writing and is in the process of writing her own memoir, which she hopes will help encourage and inspire others to heal, set themselves free to find their voice, their light and their true authentic selves. Laura is also incredibly passionate about nutrition and has studied through the Alive Academy of Natural Nutrition, receiving her diploma in Nutritional Consulting. She lives in Toronto with her cat Stripes, who is the joy and light of her life.

Facebook - https://m.facebook.com/Lauravellaactor/

Lisa Bartello

First and foremost, Lisa Bartello is a proud mother of three with a BA Honours from The University of Western Ontario. She is self-employed as a successful Realtor and Real Estate Investor. In addition, her love for helping others using her intuitive gifts and her obsession with understanding the brain and human behaviour has turned into a passionate career in teaching, guiding meditation, writing, intuitive counselling and healing modalities to re-pattern the brain so people can experience their best life. On her journey, Lisa has been known to get lucky – meeting The Long Island Medium, Theresa Caputo and Oprah, to name a few. "In every arena of my life I like to motivate and inspire people to help them realize the power lies within and they can become the highest expression of themselves and overcome any adversity."

Real Estate:

Website - www.queenrealtors.com
Facebook - Lisa Bartello Real Estate
Instagram - QueenRealtor
Twitter - @LisaturnsitSOLD
LinkedIn - Lisa Bartello

Intuitive Counselling/Teaching/Meditation Guide:

Website - www.lisabartello.ca
Facebook - Lisa Bartello (Soul Connections)
Instagram - Lisa_Bartello
Twitter - @LisaBartello
LinkedIn - Lisa Bartello

Lisa Rizzo

Lisa Rizzo is a business woman and has been blessed with the gift of being a Spiritual Medium. She started a web series called "The LINK," which broadcasts her family life and her life as a medium. She is passionate about helping others and is very close with her husband and three beautiful children. Lisa is also a writer and author, and spends her days empowering others to make their dreams come true.

Facebook - Link Lisa - https://goo.gl/L22MeU
Facebook - Community - https://goo.gl/qAL3UM

Maria Grazia Bevilacqua

Maria is a successful Doctor of Natural Medicine and an award-winning Doctor of Humanitarian Services with the World Organization of Natural Medicine. She is a highly skilled intuitive healer and a profound life coach. She is also a powerful inspirational and educational speaker who has presented in several prestigious international conferences, such as the Pacific Rim Conference in Honolulu, HI, and the Toronto Kid's Expo. Her own life experience as an owner of four natural health clinics in the GTA, and as a professional network marketer, has helped her evolve into a successful entrepreneur. Her most recent challenge was surviving a stroke, a brain aneurism and undergoing a massive brain surgery that left her partially blind. In her chapter in the first book in this series, she explains how she had made a decision to never give up, no matter what, and how she overcame the tremendous obstacles around her new disability.

Website - www.ohmnaturalhealing.com
Facebook - https://www.facebook.com/mariagrazia.bevilacqua.52

Marla David

Marla David is a retired stay-at-home Mom who gained experience through years of raising her daughters and volunteer work. In the last number of years she has attained a number of certifications, which include TESOL (Teaching English as a Second Language) from Global Leadership College, NLP Practitioner from American Union of NLP, Law of Attraction Basic Practitioner from Global Sciences Foundation, Life Coach from American Union of NLP, Ericksonian Hypnosis from American Alliance of Hypnotists, Coach in Life Optimization from The Centre for Personal Reinvention, Master Life Coach from American Union of NLP, Basic Hypnotic Communicator from Global Sciences Foundations, and Coach Practitioner from Certified Coaches Foundation. In Marla's chapter you will see how she has reaped the rewards of being a "Mom," how she has overcome obstacles, and is now living a life of passion. Marla is looking forward to the next chapter in her life, whatever it may hold. She's also hoping to use her attained skills to give back to society.

Website - http:/petluv1.wix.com
Blog - http://www.rosesandrainbows.wordpress.com
Email - Petluv1@aol.com

Minni Sharma

Minni Sharma is a registered psychotherapist, divorce and relationship specialist. Minni has been of service to her local community for over 20 years including working at a women's shelter, rape crisis centre, high schools, and hospices. She has extensive counselling experience involving individuals, youth, groups and couples experiencing divorce/separation, grief/bereavement, blended/step-families, crisis counselling, youth, cross-cultural issues, women's issues and healthy relationships.

Minni Sharma is a registered psychotherapist, divorce and relationship specialist. Minni has been of service to her local community for over 20 years, including working at a women's shelter and rape crisis centre, and in high schools and hospices. She has extensive counselling experience

involving individuals, youth, groups and couples experiencing divorce/separation, grief/bereavement, blended/step-families, crisis counselling, youth, cross-cultural issues, women's issues and healthy relationships.

Minni is also a speaker and workshop facilitator, including workshops such as "*Women in Transition-Empowering Women to Communicate.*" She enjoys travelling, meditation, and spending quality time with family and friends. She loves to laugh and enjoys exploring international cuisines. She is the proud mother of two wonderful children and is dedicated to empowering them to succeed.

Minni Sharma, Registered Psychotherapist
Website - www.guidingjourneys.ca
Email - minni@guidingjourneys.ca
Phone - 416-889-4089

Natalie Marnica

Natalie Marnica is a passionate advocate for holistic health. As a yoga therapist and teacher she believes that yoga practices should be accessible to everyone and teaches in a way that supports and empowers individuals to facilitate their own process of healing. Natalie is the founder of Sacred Mountain Yoga, which provides yoga therapy, corporate wellness programs, workshops, seminars and online training. As a person who has recovered from depression, trauma and chronic pain, Natalie believes that even in dark times there is still hope for a better future.

Website - www.smyoga.ca
Email - info@smyoga.ca
Facebook - www.facebook.com/Sacred-Mountain-Yoga
Twitter and IG @smyogini

Randi Goodman

Randi is the title author of this book. She is a caring, heart-centred entrepreneur who has led the way for women around the world. Randi is co-founder of globally renowned business conferences, including the Empowering Women to Succeed Event, Toronto Women's Expo and Business Wealth Summit. Randi has a passion for helping others. She has co-created Action Think Tank workshops and courses, as well as Innovative Living Seminars to help entrepreneurs grow their businesses; she has helped others build valuable relationships that are mutually beneficial. Randi is a fierce and fearless woman with a huge heart and dedication to teaching women and men how they can multiply their success. In her story, Randi shares the challenges of her life and how it has led her to dedicate herself to inspire and empower others.

Get a Free Audio Download on *Starting Naked; How to Win in the Game of Business…* http://www.torontowomensexpo.com

Get a Free eBook *An Introduction to Networking & Social Media Marketing Secrets* http://www.randigoodman.ca/

Websites - http://www.torontowomensexpo.com/
Websites - http://www.empoweringwomentosucceed.com
Podcast - http://empowermentradioshow.com/
Twitter - @randiconnects
Facebook - https://www.facebook.com/TorontoWomensExpo
Facebook - https://www.facebook.com/empoweringwomentosucceedewts

Sabbir Chawala

Sabbir is a real estate broker and owner with Century21 Innovative. He's been in the real estate business for six years with over 200 realtors succeeding within his brokerage. Century21 Innovative is a top 10 brokerage within Century21 in Canada. Prior to joining real estate, Sabbir worked for corporate Canada for Dell Computer and IBM as an IT business development consultant. Sabbir has over 15 years of sales/marketing experience.

Phone - 416-878-1684
Facebook - https://facebook.com/sabbir.chawala
Website - http://www.century21.ca/innovativerealty

GIFTS FOR YOU

We trust you have enjoyed the journey you've taken alongside these authors. This book was written for you to relate to, reflect on and share these real-life stories with your friends, colleagues and loved ones.

As our gift to you, go to www.empoweringwomentosucceed.com, where you will receive free electronic books from some of our authors in the first book in this series, *Empowering Women to Succeed: Tough Times Don't Last But Tough Women Do*, as well as gifts from other entrepreneurs. This is *Hundreds of Dollar$ in value!*

You will also find free downloads for *Starting Naked*, an audio book sharing how Randi Goodman got started in networking; building a business with nothing to start and now has a great following, and how you can do it too! Visit www.randigoodman.ca to download your free copy!

Finally, receive a 'start-up in social media' e-book download titled, *An Introduction to Networking & Social Media Marketing*, a new updated report that reveals some of the fastest, easiest, most profitable ways to connect with prospects, both online and offline. You will find this at www.torontowomensexpo.com.

To stay connected with our Empowering Women to Succeed community, please join us on social media, where you'll find up to date information on programs, events, courses and resources.

Join Randi's podcast here: www.empowermentradioshow.com

Follow us on Facebook here: facebook.com/empoweringwomentosuc-ceedewts

Join our community here: www.facebook.com/groups/empoweringwomentosucced/

Remember to read the first volume, *Empowering Women to Succeed: Tough Times Don't Last But Tough Women Do.* You can find it on Amazon here: http://www.empoweringwomentosucceed.com/amazon

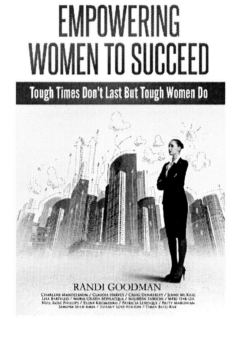